Life in the
Coral Reef

A TIME-LIFE TELEVISION BOOK

Editor: Eleanor Graves
Series Editor: Charles Osborne
Text Editor: Richard Oulahan
 Associate Text Editor: Bonnie Johnson
 Authors: Thomas A. Dozier, Don Earnest
 Assistant Editor: Peter Ainslie
 Literary Research: Ellen Schachter
 Text Research: Nancy Levering
 Copy Editors: Robert J. Myer, Greg Weed
Picture Editor: Richard O. Pollard
 Picture Research: Judith Greene
 Permissions: Cecilia Waters
Designer: Constance A. Timm
 Art Assistant: Carl Van Brunt
Production Coordinator: Jane L. Quinson

WILD, WILD WORLD OF ANIMALS
TELEVISION PROGRAM
Producers: Jonathan Donald and Lothar Wolff
This Time-Life Television Book is published by Time-Life Films, Inc.
Bruce L. Paisner, *President*
J. Nicoll Durrie, *Business Manager*

THE AUTHORS

THOMAS A. DOZIER, a foreign correspondent for *Time* and *Life* for 24 years, is the author of two volumes of this series, *Whales & Other Sea Mammals* and *Dangerous Sea Creatures*, and a contributor to two others, *Land Giants* and *The Cats*.

DON EARNEST was formerly a staff writer and editor with Time-Life Books. He has contributed to two previous volumes in this series, *Insects & Spiders* and *Birds of Field & Forest*.

THE COVER: *Synchiropus splendidus*, the richly colored, intricately marked mandarin fish, is a bottom swimmer of coral waters in the Indo-Australian seas. Inhabiting depths as low as 1,500 feet, the mandarins feed on snails and mollusks, using several rows of small, knifelike teeth to puncture the hard shells of their prey.

THE CONSULTANTS

SIDNEY HORENSTEIN is on the staff of the Department of Invertebrates, at the American Museum of Natural History, New York, and the Department of Geology and Geography, Hunter College. He has written many articles on natural history and has been a consultant on numerous Time-Life books. He publishes *New York City Notes on Natural History* and is Associate Editor of *Fossils Magazine*.

C. LAVETT SMITH is Curator and Chairman of the Department of Ichthyology at the American Museum of Natural History in New York. His research interests include the community ecology of coral reef fish and the ichthyofauna of New York State. As a diver-scientist he has studied reef fish in the Caribbean Sea and the Pacific and Indian oceans.

Wild, Wild World of Animals

Life in the
Coral Reef

Based on the television series
Wild, Wild World of Animals

Published by
TIME-LIFE FILMS

The excerpt from Mutiny on the Bounty by Charles Nordhoff and James Norman Hall, copyright 1932 by Little, Brown and Company, copyright © 1960 by Laura Nordhoff, Margaret Nordhoff Chadwick, Sarah Nordhoff McGregor, Charles Nordhoff, Jr., James Nordhoff Bunkley, Sarah M. Hall, Nancy Hall Rutgers and Conrad Hall, is reprinted by permission of Little, Brown and Company, in association with The Atlantic Monthly Press.

The excerpt from Confessions of a Beachcomber by E. J. Banfield is reprinted by permission of Ernest Benn, Ltd.

The excerpt from From Queensland to the Great Barrier Reef by Noel Monkman, copyright © 1958 by Noel Monkman, is reprinted by permission of Doubleday & Company, Inc.

The excerpt from The Ocean Island by Gilbert Klingel, copyright 1940 by Dodd, Mead & Company, Inc., copyright renewed 1968 by Gilbert Klingel, is reprinted by permission of Dodd, Mead & Company.

The excerpt from The Edge of the Sea by Rachel Carson, copyright © 1955 by Rachel L. Carson, is reprinted by permission of Marie Rodell–Francis Collin Literary Agency and Houghton Mifflin Co.

Contents

Introduction
by *Thomas A. Dozier*

FINFOOTED SNORKELERS, EXPLORING THE WONDERS OF A CORAL REEF, enter a watery world that beggars the imagination. A reef may be a petrified forest bathed in filtered sunlight, or a turreted castle bristling with stony defenses against a battering, midnight sea, or a fantastic sunken garden alive with jewellike flowers, writhing vines and vivid creatures that lurk in every crevice and cranny. The colors of a reef and the myriad marine life it harbors are a dazzling and constantly changing exercise in color dynamics. Every hue and shade imaginable may be present, from electric blues and shocking pinks to the most subtle aquatints. Yet for all its changing colors and swaying fans and fragile structure, a coral reef is an enduring geological formation that looks as if it were hewn from rock by a sea god to last for eternity. Actually, it is a prodigious creation, a living, growing, changing structure, the product of millions of hours of patient building by soft, tiny animals, some no bigger than the head of a pin.

For centuries coral reefs had been recognized as submerged menaces to shipping, but very little more was known about them. Only in fairly recent years has man come to understand something of the true nature of reefs and the minuscule architects that build them and of the complexities of the communities of marine life that depend on reefs.

Coral—the term used to designate both the animal itself and the cementlike substance it manufactures in its body to build the reef—was long believed to be a plant. In 1726 Jean André Peyssonel, a French naturalist, discovered that coral is instead an animal belonging to the phylum of coelenterates, which also includes jellyfish, sea anemones and hydroids. Like the other coelenterates, coral is a very simple organism, a tiny, transparent, gelatinous body enclosed in a tube with an opening at one end. Around the opening, which functions both as a mouth and as a passage to excrete wastes, is a fringe of tiny tentacles. These gather in the little animal's food and give it its other common name, polyp, from the Greek word meaning "many-footed." Polyp corals live entirely on tiny plankton, that abundant soup of minute plants and animals that nourishes so many sea creatures from whales to tiny animals.

Polyps are true hermaphrodites, capable of producing either sperm or eggs at different times and also of reproducing themselves by a nonsexual process called budding. In the role of a male, a polyp expels sperm cells into the sea, where they may fertilize free-floating eggs or be ingested by another polyp—temporarily female—to fertilize the eggs within its body. When the eggs are ready to hatch, the polyp contracts its sides, and newborn coral animals are spewed forth in great numbers. The young planulae, as they are called, are equipped with small, whiplike hairs that allow them to swim until they reach a suitable anchorage—usually the reef, a rock or other hard surface. Some polyps simply grow buds, knobby protuberances on their bodies, which become new, living creatures exactly like the parent. These budded offspring are created without resort to eggs, sperm or fertilization and without the risk swimming planulae face in hostile waters, filled with predators. In budding, polyps do not break off and swim away. They simply sprout from the parent, begin to build their own exoskeletons and in turn grow buds that in time become new polyps themselves, each enlarging the coral mass with seemingly infinite capabilities for reproducing itself.

In contrast to jellyfish and some other coelenterates, which are free-moving wander-

Retreating waves expose a windward reef near Wuvulu Island off the coast of New Guinea in the Bismarck Archipelago.

Coral reefs can exist only in tropical and subtropical waters and are
confined to a narrow girdle around the earth's midsection, extending just
30 degrees north and south of the Equator, as shown on the map below.
Reefs take three forms: fringe reefs, which are shelflike extensions of the
shore itself; barrier reefs, walls of coral that are separated from coastal
littorals by lagoons that may range in width from a few yards to 150 miles,
and atolls, circlets of coral that grow around tropical islands or lagoons
formed by sunken islands, often located in mid-ocean and rising
thousands of feet from the bottom of the sea.

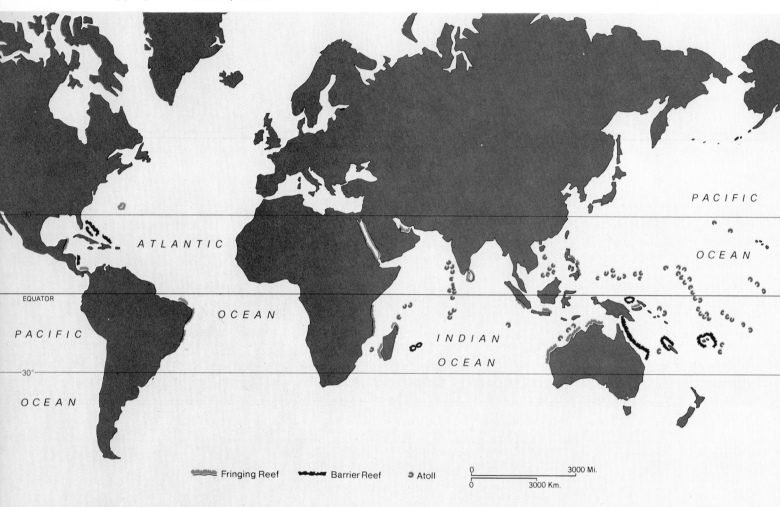

Fringing Reef   Barrier Reef   Atoll

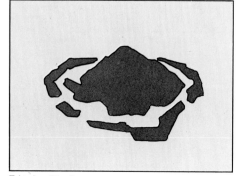

Fringing Reef

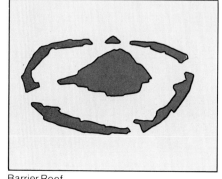

Barrier Reef

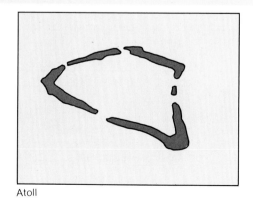

Atoll

10

ers through the waters all their lives, the stony polyp is stationary for most of its life. It anchors itself permanently and, extracting calcium carbonate from the seawater, begins the process of constructing an external skeleton of hard limestone, which is the raw material for the reef. The polyp wraps most of its body in this very tough and long-lasting mineral substance—and that is how coral reefs come into existence.

For about half a billion years, generation after generation of these industrious builders have been constructing coral reefs by the simple process of wrapping themselves in their limestone refuges. When a polyp dies its soft inner body and fringing tentacles decay, leaving the rocklike outer skeleton, which has been joined by thousands of similiar polyp casings and in time will be united with millions more. Thus despite the fact that coral reefs are subject to destruction by the elements and various living creatures that feed upon or dissolve the limestone, coral reefs are now scattered over an estimated 70 million square miles of sea bottom. This is an area approximately 20 times larger than the entire continental United States. The greatest of all reefs is the Great Barrier Reef off the northeast coast of Australia, which stretches at an average undersea height of 500 feet for 1,260 miles. This stupendous submarine redoubt is the largest single structure ever built by living creatures, dwarfing in comparison all the mightiest works of man: the pyramids of ancient Egypt, the stone fortresses of pre-Columbian America, the cathedrals of Europe, the towering skyscrapers of the 20th century's urban centers.

Another impressive concentration of coral structures is in the Red Sea, which is lined by reefs along its 1,300 miles of length. Other major reefs occur in the Indian Ocean, in the Bahamas and in the equatorial Pacific. The location of their sites on a globe supplies a clue to the basic requirements of reef-building corals: shallow, clear, sunlit tropical waters with a minimum temperature of around 70° F. Such conditions are found only in a belt extending around the earth's midsection, bounded by latitudes 30 degrees north and south of the Equator. Some 2,500 species of corals live in every ocean and sea at varying latitudes, depths and temperatures. But the reef builders depend on the algae that dwell within the polyp's tissues to rid them of wastes, including carbon dioxide, in order to thrive and grow, and the algae in turn need sunlight to live. Reefs are almost never found on the western coastlines of either continents or islands. This is because the direction of the earth's rotation on its axis causes colder water to be swept upward from the depths on the western shores of land masses, and the hard corals cannot build reefs in cold water or depths much greater than about 150 feet. The clear, clean nature of tropical waters is necessary not only to permit the light to filter through but also to keep the polyp from being smothered in mud and other sediment. Included among the polyp's other environmental needs are these: restless, moving water on the exposed, seaward side of the reef that not only provides added oxygen but, in addition, helps sweep food within range of the immobile animal's gently undulating tentacles.

Given these requirements of living coral, the 500-foot depth plumbed by the foundations of the Great Barrier Reef seems a mystery. Even more perplexing, it would appear, are the countless coral atolls and islands rising from the sea floor many thousands of feet below the surface. In 1837 the great naturalist Charles Darwin advanced an explanation for these riddles that has stood the tests of time and modern scientific experiment. When Darwin began his studies, exploration had already shown that there are three basic types of coral reefs: the fringing reef, which spreads out laterally and contiguously from the land in shallow inshore waters; the barrier reef, a formation that may lie a mile or more off shore, separated from the land by a deep, placid lagoon; and the atoll, a coral ring in the open sea, encircling a lagoon. With the help of windblown vegetation, atolls sometimes grow into sizable, fertile islands supporting human populations.

The existence of fringing reefs needed the least explanation, since their foundations are well within the 150-foot average depth required by the coral polyp. But to Darwin's contemporaries, the barrier reef and the atolls presented a scientific enigma, for their foundations lay hundreds and even thousands of feet deeper. Darwin's solution was called the subsidence theory. He reasoned that since the earth's crust is constantly if almost imperceptibly rising and falling, all coral reefs were originally fringing reefs and that the sea bed subsided more or less at the same rate that coral builders added new limestone near the surface. Even with a very gradual falling of the ocean floor the original corals of the reef would eventually sink beneath the 150-foot maximum depth, but by that time they would be long dead; their descendants would still be building in shallow surface waters above, adding to the limestone foundations formed by ancestral corals. In theory there would be no limit to the distance between a barrier reef's living upper stories and its fossilized underpinnings, so long as the builders kept pace with the gradual subsidence of the sea floor.

The same theory explains the mystery of the coral atoll rising thousands of feet from the ocean floor. A series of 19th-century exploratory drillings into atolls showed the presence of coral-formed limestone as deep as 1,114 feet, apparently proving Darwin's theory. Further support came in 1947 when a group of scientists drilled 2,556 feet into Bikini Atoll, a submerged skyscraper in the Pacific, and brought up typically shallow-water reef material. Efforts were continued to reach the bottom of the coral and find out exactly what lay beneath. They succeeded in 1952 at Eniwetok, just before that Pacific atoll became the site of the world's first hydrogen-bomb explosion. Working against a deadline set by the nuclear testers, a group of American geologists finally pierced the coral overlay at 4,222 feet and reached basalt, a hard rock of volcanic origin. The geologists concluded that the atoll, made up of thousands of feet of coral skeletons, rested on a base of volcanic rock that had once been about 150 feet below the surface of the sea. And they calculated that Eniwetok had been sinking at an average rate of .04 of an inch per century for the past 60 million years.

Besides offering a fascinating area of exploration for marine geologists, coral reefs are the homes of vast and variegated communities of sea animals that shelter in the protection of the reef and find sustenance there in the form of other marine animals and

A fringing reef extends from the shore of an island in the Dahlak Archipelago in the Red Sea.

vegetation. The coral community harbors a population of many thousand different species, ranging in size from creatures so small they cannot be seen with the naked eye to huge sharks which, although not permanent tenants of the reef, are frequent visitors because of the almost infinite variety of prey to be found there. For the same reason, silvery barracudas use the reefs as hunting preserves. Stingrays and deadly poisoners like the stonefish lurk on the bottom, and the spectacular manta ray flies through the tranquil water of the leeward sides of reefs on its extended wings. The starfish, whose coloration is as varied as its arm count (most have five, but some have 45 or more), clings to the coral reef, a threat to slow-moving prey and the reef itself, which some species eat with apparent relish. There are mollusks by the dozens, many of them growing to extraordinary size—giant 500-pound clams and seven-pound oysters—because of the abundant food in the reef.

The true bony-spined fish of the reef are generally, except for the great visiting predators, small, fast, graceful and brilliantly colored. They are probably the most varied in species and colors of all the creatures of the reef, which they share with the crustaceans—lobsters, shrimps and crabs among them. These live both in deep water and in tidal pools on the shoreline. Some have emerged from the water altogether and make their homes on the beach, itself a by-product of the reef. The fine white sand is made up of coral beaten to powder by waves or pulverized by coral-eating animals.

Such a rich store of edible resources available on the beach and in the shallow water of the reef naturally attracts legions of shore birds: herons, silver gulls, noddy terns, boobies, sooty terns, shearwaters. The aquatic fowl population on the islands of the Great Barrier Reef numbers in the millions. Reef beaches are also the nesting places for the oceangoing green turtle, which laboriously crawls from the water, struggles through the sand to a site well above the highest tide and digs a hole in which to deposit her eggs, as many as 200 at a time, as often as seven times in a breeding season. In the chambered recesses of the

Clouds part to reveal a breathtaking aerial view of one of the Society Islands in the South Pacific and the barrier reef that almost completely encircles its coastline.

14

reef and the crystal-clear water around it the sea dwellers live out their lives in competition as well as in symbiotic relationships with their fellow tenants: commensalism, where different species coexist without either helping or harming the others; and the marvelous relationship of mutualism, with creatures of widely different kinds living together for mutual help and protection. In the symbiotic *modus vivendi* of the reef are some of the most unusual cooperative arrangements in all the animal kingdom.

One fascinating and puzzling symbiotic relationship is that of the venomous sea anemone with the gentle, white-striped clownfish. Most creatures of the clownfish's size that venture near the anemone's envenomed tentacles are immediately paralyzed. But the piscine clown is immune and makes its home in the midst of the treacherously graceful waving arms; the anemone amiably permits its guest to dart in and out of its mouth to scavenge morsels of undigested meat from its stomach. Scientists are not in complete agreement about what reciprocal service the clownfish performs, but most believe that it lures larger prey within range of the anemone's tentacles.

A more curious symbiotic relationship exists between the tiny goby fish and certain coral reef shrimp. The two share a common sea-bed hole as living quarters, and the goby acts as a seeing-eye fish to the half-blind shrimp, which establishes contact by touching the fish with its sensitive antennae, while the goby responds by signaling approaching danger with wriggling movements of its two-inch body.

The complex interrelationships between the animals and plants of the coral reef have resulted in a watery ecological order that is the equal of any that exists on the land. But even in its seeming security beneath the waves, the world of the coral reef is threatened by man and his works. Oil spills, detergents and other pollutants and the encroachment of overfishing are all potential destroyers. As awareness of these dangers grows, the hope is that the reefs will escape the fate of so many terrestrial environments and survive in all their splendor.

Washed by the waters of the Indian Ocean, some 2,000 miles northwest of Australia, is North Keeling Island, a typical ring-shaped atoll surrounding a shallow, sandy-bottomed lagoon.

Corals and Anemones

Because their rippling tentacles resemble windblown flowers, corals have been given the name of Anthozoa, or "flower animals." In fact, for centuries naturalists classified the tiny creatures as plants. Like flowers themselves, the anthozoans come in many spectacular varieties. The true corals are divided, with a few exceptions, into two orders: soft corals, or alcyonarians, and hard or stony corals, appropriately called madrepores, or mothers-of-stone. All the reef builders, which number some 650 out of more than 2,500 species of coral, are madrepores and can build their great stone structures only in tropical waters and at an average depth of 150 feet below the surface. Other corals, both hard and soft, live in all kinds of submarine habitats all over the world, including the frigid waters of the sub-Arctic regions. In those areas beyond the tropic zones where they exist, however, madrepores are unable to build reefs. Soft corals live in colonies on the ocean floor and sometimes on the reefs themselves, where they contribute indirectly to the building process, leaving their skeletons as bricks for the madrepores' mortar as part of the detritus that becomes affixed to the reef formation.

The principal anatomical differences between stony and soft corals are the degree of hardness of their skeletons and the number of tentacles and radial partitions dividing the minuscule cups where the coral polyp lives. Soft corals have hornlike, flexible skeletons and eight partitions and grow branched tentacles in series of eight. The madrepores usually sprout branched or unbranched tentacles in multiples of six and have six partitions. All corals are armed with stings on their tentacles, which they use to immobilize the tiny animals, or zooplankton, that make up a large part of their diet.

Among the most common of coral formations that go into the basic structure of a reef are the huge elkhorn corals, which take their name from the resemblance to the flattened antlers of the elk. They are formed when polyps bud from their parents and build outward in haphazard directions, in much the same way that the points of an elk's antlers grow. The top of this network often grows to within a few inches of the surface and at low tide is briefly exposed to the air but only in between the big waves that constantly wash over it. Elkhorn corals are found on the exposed face of a reef, as they are thick and strong enough to withstand the full force of deep-sea storms.

Staghorn coral is a related antlerlike form. But it achieves a greater elegance of shape and structural delicacy because it is built by its tiny ever-multiplying tenants in calmer and deeper waters where it can flourish undisturbed by the open sea's winds and waves. It is brittle, and, like elkhorns, staghorns contribute their dead skeletons to the underpinnings of the reef, though they do not form part of the interior structure. Both staghorn and elkhorn corals of the West Indies are a yellow-brown color. In the Pacific reefs the antler forms are more colorful.

Less colorful but more important in reef building are the enormous boulderlike corals, exemplified by the brain coral. It is so named because the twisting ridges and valleys left by the stringlike polyps that build and inhabit it make the stone closely resemble a mammalian brain. It is one of the biggest of all coral structures, reaching 12 to 15 feet in diameter and often weighing several tons. The star coral is another boulder-type formation that grows to great size. It takes its name from the small partitions within the calcareous cup of the living polyp's home. Called *septa*, these form perfect star patterns and stud the mother stone like tiny medallions.

All the massive and extensive coral madrepores—the elkhorn, the brain, the star and many others—are the foundation stones and buttresses of coral reefs. Most of the external decorations are provided by the soft corals, the alcyonarians, which come in a wide variety of fantastic forms and colors, and most are named for familiar objects that they resemble. The multibranched gorgonians, named for the three sisters of Greek mythology who had writhing snakes for hair, include some of the most beautiful corals. The sea fans, firmly rooted to the reef floor, consist of a series of flattened tubes, each containing hundreds of polyps, filagreed by crisscrossed horizontal ribs.

Sea anemones are first cousins to corals but do not secrete limestone and, like many of the soft corals, take no part in building the reef. Although considerably bigger than individual coral polyps, they have much the same anatomical structure. They consist of hollow tubes with mouths and stinging tentacles at one end. Their tentacles grow in dense masses and mimic the petals of a flower more closely than any other "flower animals." They wave enticingly and beautifully in all the vivid colors of nature's palette: purple, pink, bright blue, red, green, yellow. Once a small, vulnerable fish, crab or shrimp comes within range, the anemone's arms reach out, gather in the victim, immobilize it and shove it through the mouth in the center of its magnificent floral clusters.

Staghorn, elkhorn and gorgonian coral

The Builders

The reef builders are all true or stony corals. All have similar polyps that resemble fragile anemones and are housed in cuplike structures of limestone. The polyps may be widely separated in individual cups or placed so close together as to share common walls. Or, as in the case of brain coral (opposite), polyps are joined to form long, convoluted paths between continuous meandering rows of tentacles. Of the few corals that are solitary, the mushroom coral, *Fungia* (above), is the largest. The mushroom's single brownish green polyp often grows to a diameter of five inches; it has tentacles that, when extended, protrude another two or three inches.

The treelike species of corals, such as the staghorn and elkhorn corals (overleaf), make a major contribution to the construction of the reefs. Among other corals that produce massive growths are members of the genus *Porites*, one species of which forms large, rounded fingerlike projections (right). Although each polyp of *Porites* is less than one tenth of an inch in diameter, they join to build blocks that measure as much as 20 feet across. It has been estimated that such a coral mound takes its tiny builders over 200 years to construct.

The fragile intertwined stalks above are "antlers" of staghorn coral; the sturdier branches at right are elkhorn coral. Members of the genus Acropora, both are major coral builders, sometimes comprising as much as 75 percent of a reef. Their ability as constructors is due, in part, to their rapid growth rate. Growth in staghorn coral is estimated to be as much as two inches a year.

Common Denominator

Despite the tremendous variety among the 2,500 different species of corals, they share one basic characteristic. All are the creations of tiny sea animals called polyps that are shaped like cylinders. One end is attached to a permanent anchorage; the other is formed into a flattened disk encompassing an oval slit of a mouth. Around this disk sprout one or more circles of tentacles, delicate feelers that collect the creature's planktonic food.

During the day most of these minuscule reef inhabitants fold up their tentacles and hide, as seen in the coral on the opposite page. As the light begins to fade, the feathery tentacles emerge to snare the plankton that is especially abundant at night. When their tentacles unfurl, as in the coral below with a red sponge attached to it, the polyps are able to grasp such prey as minute crustaceans—or, in the larger species, even small fish—and drop it into their mouths. With hundreds of fragile fingers extended for the feast, the exterior of a coral reef takes on a furry appearance.

The Last of the Pandora

by Charles Nordhoff and James Norman Hall

Although Midshipman Roger Byam was an innocent bystander and an unwilling participant in the famous mutiny aboard H.M.S. Bounty in 1789, he was regarded as a nefarious mutineer by the captain of the British vessel Pandora, who arrested him in Tahiti. Byam was taken aboard Pandora in chains, to be returned to England for court-martial. His voyage in the ship's hold is a tale of unmitigated horror, but when the ship foundered on a coral reef in the South Seas, the unfortunate young man found himself caught up in a nightmare. The following selection from Nordhoff and Hall's Mutiny on the Bounty describes the terrible, grinding destruction of the ship.

The twenty-eighth of August was a dismal day of alternate calms and black squalls which greatly increased the dangers of navigation. Looking from my knot-hole at dawn, I saw that we were in the midst of a labyrinth of reefs and shoals upon which the sea broke with great violence. The frigate had been hove-to during the night, and now one of the boats, with Lieutenant Corner in command, had gone ahead to seek for a possible passage. We could see little of what was taking place, but the orders continually shouted from the quarter-deck indicated only too clearly the difficulties in which the ship found herself. Once, as we were about, we passed within half a cable's length of as villainous a reef as ever brought a sailor's heart into his mouth.

So it went all that day, and as evening drew on it was apparent that we were in greater danger than we had been at dawn. The launch was still far in advance of us, and a gun was fired as a signal for her to return. Darkness fell swiftly. False fires were burned and muskets fired to indi-cate our position to the launch. The musket fire was answered from the launch, and as the reports became more distinct we knew that she was slowly approaching. All this while the leadsmen were continually sounding, finding no bottom at one hundred and ten fathoms; but soon we heard them calling depths again: fifty fathoms, forty, thirty-six, twenty-two. Immediately upon calling this latter depth the ship was put about, but before the tacks were hauled on board and the sails trimmed, the frigate struck, and every man in the roundhouse was thrown sprawling to the length of his chain.

Before we could recover ourselves the ship struck again, with such force that we thought the masts would come down. It was now pitch-dark, and to make matters worse another heavy squall bore down upon us. Above the roaring of the wind we could hear the voices of the men, sounding faint and thin as orders were shouted. Every effort was made to get the ship free by means of the sails, but, this failing, they were furled and the other boats put over the side for the purpose of carrying out an anchor. The squall passed as suddenly as it had come, and we now heard distinctly the musket shots of the men in the returning launch.

The violence of the shocks we had received left no doubt in our minds that the ship had been badly damaged. I heard Edwards's voice: "How does she do, Mr. Roberts?" and Roberts's reply: "She's making water fast, sir. There's nearly three feet in the hold."

The effect upon the prisoners of this dreadful news may be imagined. Hillbrandt and Michael Byrne began to cry aloud in piteous voices, begging those outside to release us

from our irons. All our efforts to quiet them were useless, and the clamour they made, with the tumult of shouting outside and the thunder of the surf on the reef where we lay, added to the terror and gloom of the situation.

Hands were immediately turned to the pumps, and orders were given that other men should bail at the hatchways. Presently the grating over the roundhouse scuttle was unlocked and the master-at-arms entered with a lantern. He quickly unshackled Coleman, Norman, and McIntosh, and ordered them on deck to lend a hand. We begged the master-at-arms to release all of us, but he gave no heed, and when he had gone out with the three men the iron grating was replaced and locked as before.

Some of the prisoners now began to rave and curse like madmen, wrenching at their chains in the vain effort to break them. At this time Edwards appeared at the scuttle and sternly ordered us to be silent.

"For God's sake, unshackle us, sir!" Muspratt called. "Give us a chance for our lives!"

"Silence! Do you hear me?" Edwards replied; then, to the master-at-arms, who stood beside him by the scuttle: "Mr. Jackson, I hold you responsible for the prisoners. They are not to be loosed without my orders."

"Let us bear a hand at the pumps, sir," Morrison called, earnestly.

"Silence, you villains!" Edwards called, and with that he left us.

Realizing now that pleading was useless, the men quieted down, and we resigned ourselves to the situation in that mood of hopeless apathy that comes over men powerless to help themselves. Within an hour another tempest of wind and rain struck us, and again the frigate was lifted by the seas and battered with awful violence on the reef. These repeated shocks threw us from side to side and against the walls and each other, so that we were dreadfully cut and bruised. As nearly as we could judge, the ship was being carried farther and farther across the reef. At length she lay quiet, down by the head, and we heard Lieutenant Corner's voice: "She's clear, sir!"

It must then have been about ten o'clock. The second squall had passed, and in the silence that followed the screaming of the wind we could plainly hear the orders being given. The guns were being heaved over the side, and the men who could be spared from bailing and pumping were employed in thrumbing a topsail to haul under the ship's bottom, in an endeavor to fother her. But the leak gained so fast that this plan had to abandoned, and every man on board, with the exception of our guards and ourselves, fell to bailing and pumping.

Edwards's conduct toward us is neither to be explained nor excused. The reef upon which the *Pandora* had struck was leagues distant from any land, with the exception of a few small sand-bars and stretches of barren rock. Had we been free, there would have been no possibility of escape; and yet Edwards doubled the guard over the roundhouse and gave orders to the master-at-arms to keep us chained hand and foot. Fortunately, we did not realize the imminence of our danger. The roundhouse being on the quarterdeck, we were high above the water, and while we knew that the ship was doomed, we did not know that the leak was gaining so rapidly. It was, in fact, a race between the sea and daylight, and had the frigate gone down in the

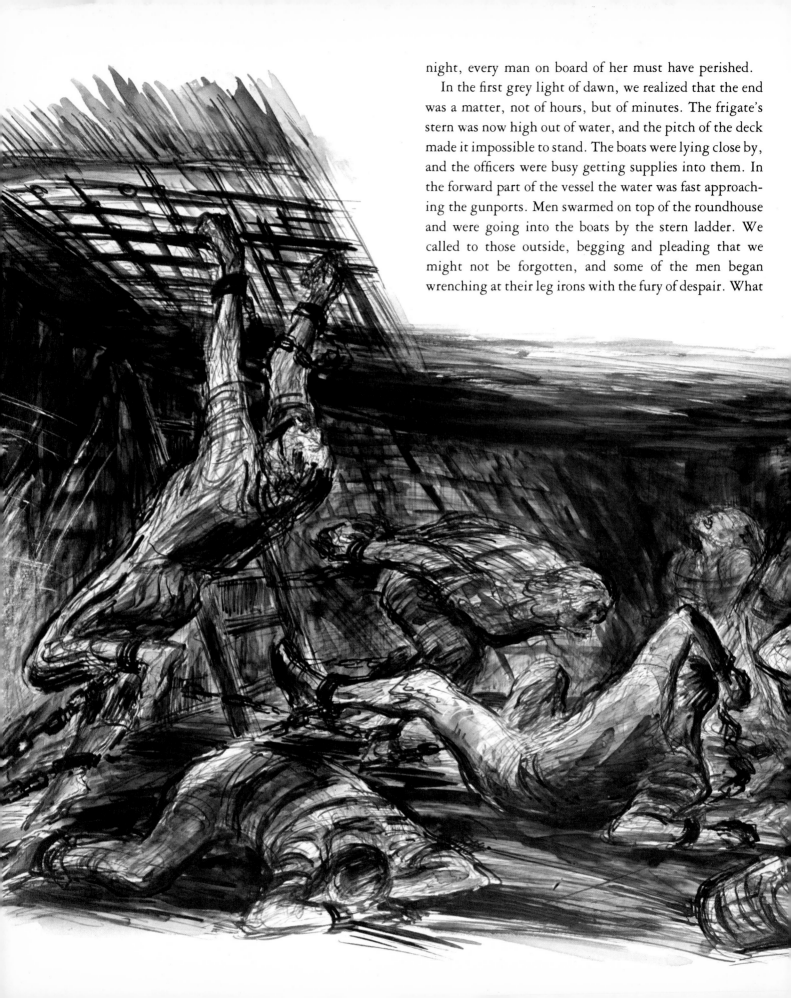

night, every man on board of her must have perished.

In the first grey light of dawn, we realized that the end was a matter, not of hours, but of minutes. The frigate's stern was now high out of water, and the pitch of the deck made it impossible to stand. The boats were lying close by, and the officers were busy getting supplies into them. In the forward part of the vessel the water was fast approaching the gunports. Men swarmed on top of the roundhouse and were going into the boats by the stern ladder. We called to those outside, begging and pleading that we might not be forgotten, and some of the men began wrenching at their leg irons with the fury of despair. What the orders respecting us were, or whether any had been given, I know not, but our entreaties must have been heard by those outside. Joseph Hodges, the armourer's mate, came down to us and removed the irons of Byrne, Muspratt, and Skinner; but Skinner, in his eagerness to get out, was hauled up with his handcuffs on, the two other men following close behind. Then the scuttle was closed and barred again. This was done, I believe, by the order of Lieutenant Parkin, for a moment before I had seen him peering down at us.

Hodges had not noticed that the scuttle had been closed. He was unlocking our irons as rapidly as possible

when the ship gave a lurch and there was a general cry of "There she goes!" Men were leaping into the water from the stern, for the boats had pushed off at the first appearance of motion in the ship. We shouted with all our strength, for the water was beginning to flow in upon us. That we were not all drowned was due to the humanity of James Moulter, the boatswain's mate. He had scrambled up on the roof of the roundhouse in order to leap into the sea, and, hearing our cries, he replied that he would either set us free or go to the bottom with us. He drew out the bars that fastened the scuttle to the coamings, and heaved the scuttle overboard. "Hasten, lads!" he cried, and then himself leaped into the sea.

In his excitement and fear, the armourer's mate had neglected to remove the handcuffs of Burkitt and Hillbrandt, although they were free of their leg irons. We scrambled out, helping each other, and not a moment too soon. The ship was under water as far as the mainmast, and I saw Captain Edwards swimming toward the pinnace, which was at a considerable distance. I leaped from the stern and had all I could do to clear myself from the driver boom before the ship went down. I swam with all my strength and was able to keep beyond the suction of the water as the stern of the frigate rose perpendicularly and slid into the sea. Few seamen know how to swim, and the cries of drowning men were awful beyond the power of words to describe. All hatch covers, spare booms, the coops for fowls, and the like, had been cut loose, and some of the men had succeeded in reaching floating articles; but others went down almost within reach of planks or booms that might have saved them. I swam to one of the hatch covers and found Muspratt at the other end. He was unable to swim, but told me that he could hang on until he should be picked up. I swam to a short plank, and, with this to buoy me, started in the direction of one of the boats. I had been in the water nearly an hour before I was taken up by the blue yawl. Of the prisoners, Ellison and Byrne had been rescued by this boat, which was now filled with men, and we set out for a small sandy key on the reef at a distance of about three miles from where the ship went down. This was the only bit of land above water anywhere about, although there were shoals on every side near enough to the surface for the sea to break over them.

There was quiet water at the key, which was nearly encircled by reef, and we had no difficulty in landing. As soon as the men were disembarked, with such provision as the boat contained, the yawl was sent back to the scene of the wreck. Ellison, Byrne, and I were kept at the oars, and Bowling, the master's mate, was at the tiller. We made a wide search among floating wreckage, and so strong were the currents thereabout that we took up men as far as three miles from the reef where the ship had struck. We rescued twelve in all, among them Burkitt, clinging to a spar with his handcuffs still on his wrists.

It was nearly midday before we returned to the key, and by that time the other boats had assembled there. The sand-bar, for it was no more than that, was about thirty paces long by twenty wide. Nothing grew there—not a sprig of green to relieve the eyes from the blinding glare of the sun. Captain Edwards ordered a muster of the survivors, and it was found that thirty-three of the ship's company and four of the prisoners had been drowned. Of the prisoners, Stewart, Sumner, Hillbrandt, and Skinner were missing.

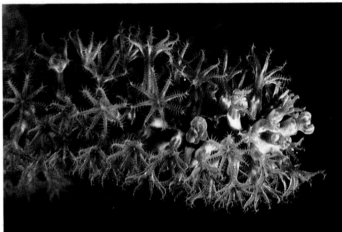

Flexible Corals

To the diver sightseeing in the reef's coral gardens, the most striking visions are the soft corals, whose delicate shapes have earned them such names as sea fans, sea plumes and sea whips. Formed with flexible skeletons instead of stony structures, they may branch outward like the scarlet sea fan (upper picture, above) or throw out snaky tendrils as shown at left; others shoot upward like the waving sea whips (opposite), which grow taller than a man. These expansive shapes give each tiny member of such animal colonies maximum exposure to the edible material in the water; the food is gathered by the open polyps on the tip of a sea whip (above, bottom). Partly as a result of their efficient eating habits, soft corals abound everywhere on the reef.

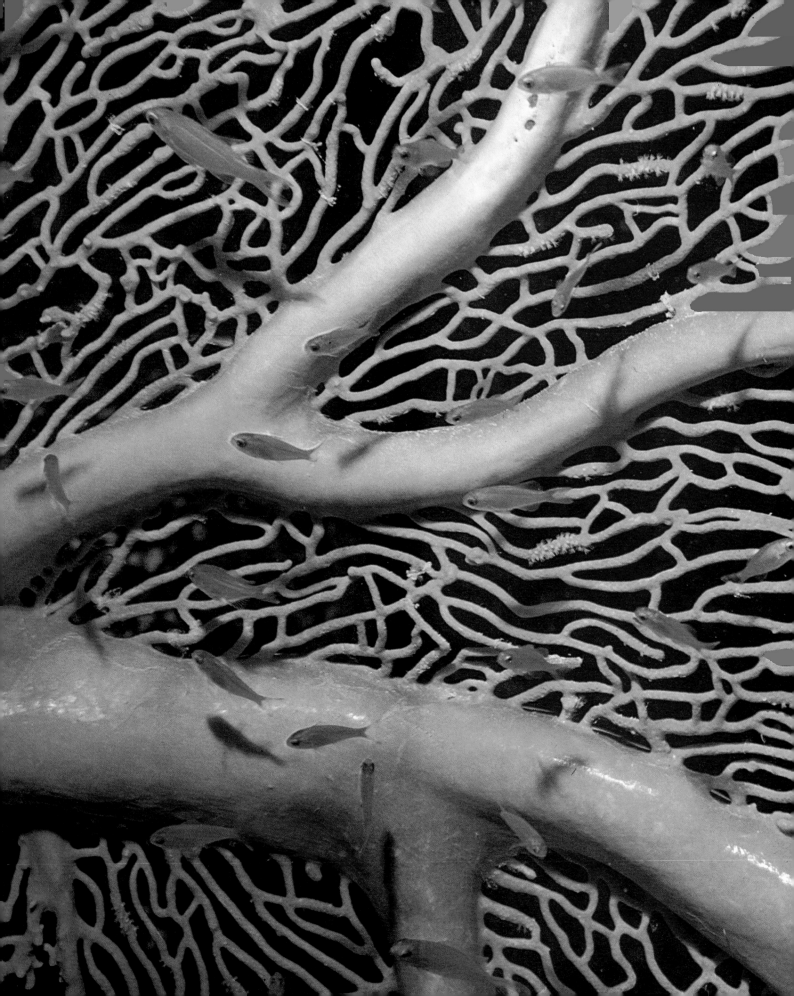

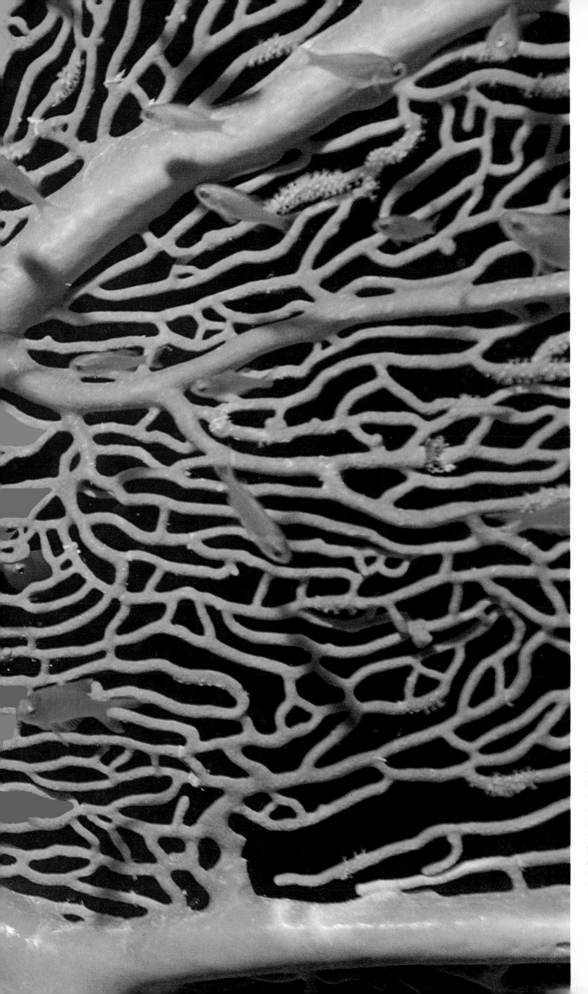

In this greatly enlarged view of the lacy crossribs of a flame-colored sea fan, a score of luminous purple fish create a startling contrast of colors. But to the eyes of most predators the tiny fish appear to be so well camouflaged that they blend unobtrusively into the soft coral background.

Confessions of a Beachcomber

by E. J. Banfield

As any old salt knows, a coral reef is a place of menacing danger, a ship's graveyard that must be treated with wary respect. But to a neophyte skindiver, a reef seems to be a world of surpassing beauty, innocence and tranquillity. E. J. Banfield, author of My Tropic Island, *has made a closer inspection of reefs, taking the point of view of the inhabitants, and he has uncovered a raging battlefield, which he describes here, in a selection from his* Confessions of a Beachcomber.

A coral reef is gorged with a population of varied elements viciously disposed towards each othèr. It is one of Nature's most cruel battlefields, for it is the brood of the sea that "plots mutual slaughter, hungering to live." Molluscs are murderers and the most shameless of cannibals. No creature at all conspicuous is safe, unless it is agile and alert, or of horrific aspect, or endowed with giant's strength, or is encased in armour. A perfectly inoffensive crab, incapable of inflicting injury to anything save creatures of almost microscopic dimensions, assumes the style and demeanour of a ferocious monster, ready at a moment's notice to cry havoc, and let loose the dogs of war. Another hides itself as a rugged nodule of moss-covered stone; its limbs so artfully stowed away that detection would be impossible did it not occasionally betray itself by a stealthy

movement. The pretty cowrie, lemon-coloured and grey and brown, throws over its shining shoulders a shawl of the hue of the rock on which it crawls about, grey or brown or tawny, with white specks and dots which make for invisibility—a thin filmy shawl of exquisite sensitiveness. Touch it ever so lightly, and the helpless creature, discerning that its disguise has been penetrated, withdraws it, folding it into its shell, and closes its door against expected attack. It may feebly fall off the rock, and simulating a dead and empty shell, lie motionless until danger is past. Then again it will drape itself in its garment of invisibility and slide cautiously along in search of its prey. Under the loose rocks and detached lumps of coral for one live there will be scores of dead shells. The whole field is strewn with the relics of perpetual conflict, resolving and being re-solved into original elements. We talk of the strenuous life of men in cities. Go to a coral reef and see what the struggle for existence really means. The very bulwarks of limestone are honeycombed by tunnelling shells. A glossy black, torpedo-shaped creature cuts a tomb for itself in the hard lime. Though it may burrow inches deep with no readily visible inlet, cutting and grinding its cavity as it develops in size and strength, yet it is not safe. Fate follows in insignificant guise, drills a tiny hole through its shell, and the toilsomely excavated refuge becomes a sepulchre. Even in the fastness of the coral "that grim sergeant death is strict in his arrest." All is strife—war to the death. If eternal vigilance is the price of liberty among men, what quality shall avert destruction where insatiable cannibalism is the rule.

Feather Dusters

Looking like nothing so much as a vibrantly colored feather duster stuck into the sea floor, the multi-armed creatures at left and below are actually tube coral and cup coral, respectively. Both are members of the order Alcyonaria, commonly called soft corals. Instead of producing the limy skeletons of the true or stony corals, most of these soft corals secrete a horny substance in the form of small rods that are scattered, sometimes quite loosely, throughout the entire organism, giving it a flexible texture rather than the rigid façade of reef coral.

The alcyonarians are characterized by polyps that have tentacles that always grow in multiples of eight. Like all other members of their order, the soft corals' tentacles are lined with stinging cells, or nematocysts. But these are so small in soft corals that they can be safely handled.

Flowers of Death

Named for the showy red and purple windflowers, sea anemones, such as the lavender specimen below, look more like prized dahlias or chrysanthemums. Beautiful and fragile though they may appear, sea anemones are death traps for most small creatures that may brush against a waving tentacle. Each translucent tip contains a stinger that immediately stuns and immobilizes a victim, which is quickly passed from tentacle to tentacle with the efficiency of a fireman's bucket brigade and shoved into the creature's gaping mouth. In the photograph of an Atlantic curlycue anemone on the opposite page, the mouth appears as an open vortex among the swirling, saffron-colored tendrils.

Sea Stars

After dark, when many of the fish retire, a night shift of quieter creatures emerges from hiding places under coral boulders or from niches in the reef's eroded caverns. Among these are the starfish and their relatives. Constellations of them dot the flat bottoms between the coral ridges as soon as the sun goes down.

Members of the echinoderm phylum, starfish—more properly known as sea stars—vary considerably. In form they range from creatures with slender tubular arms resembling a hub with spokes to the more familiar star shapes to armless pentagons. Five arms are most common, but many stars have 10, 13, 20 or even 45. From tip to tip, reef starfish average a foot in diameter, but some bug-sized sea stars are small enough to make their daytime homes in the pores of sponges, and the giant *Oreaster*, an ocean dweller that frequently grazes on coral flats, often measures 20 inches across. Their colors range from brilliant scarlets, oranges and purples to more subtle mottled rusts and creamy yellows.

The diet of these carnivorous animals is equally varied. Many eat snails, worms, anemones, sea urchins and smaller stars. Some even eat small fish and shrimp. Few will pass up a free meal of carrion. But nearly all exhibit a special preference for bivalves, such as clams, oysters, scallops and mussels. And the way that some sea stars pry open the tightly clamped shells is one of the more amazing feats of strength in the animal kingdom. Under each arm a sea star has two or more rows of tubular feet tipped with suckers that operate by water pressure. Attacking a bivalve, the sea star wraps itself around the shellfish, positioning its mouth over the tight seam between the shells. Then with its suckers it pulls on the shells with a force of up to 10 pounds. When even the tiniest slit appears, the sea star quickly turns its stomach inside out through its mouth and inserts it through the gap. The oyster or clam inside is done for. An assault by starfish on an oyster bed can spell disaster to the mollusks and commercial ruin for oystermen.

The eating habits of one giant sea star—the crown-of-thorns—have earned it a notoriety unmatched among reef dwellers. In the 1960s these once rare sea stars began appearing in large numbers. Their proliferation raised fears for the survival of all the coral reefs in the Indian and Pacific oceans. With from 11 to 23 arms densely covered with prickly spines, the aptly named crown-of-thorns eats the delicate polyps of the coral itself. But unlike other polyp eaters that selectively nibble and leave enough living coral to regenerate, this sea star strips the coral so efficiently that only a bare white skeleton of dead coral remains. Since each star denudes about seven square feet of coral a week, the thousands that may gather to feed on the same reef can devastate miles of coral in short order. In two and a half years a scourge of crown-of-thorns destroyed nearly all of the living polyps along a 24-mile stretch of reef in Guam, and over a quarter of Australia's 1,200-mile Great Barrier Reef is now endangered.

To save the reefs, naturalists have donned wet suits and with underwater searchlights have tried to find and eradicate the brambly-looking starfish. But their efforts have been limited by the crown-of-thorns' remarkable powers of regeneration. The animal cannot simply be chopped up, for, like all sea stars, it can regrow an entire body from just one piece.

Efforts have also been made to find the causes of the population explosions. Man-made pollution, such as sewage, has been blamed for creating surplus nutrients for the starfish; so have the shell collectors who strip the reef of the colorful triton snail, the sea star's principal predator. However, in 1970 a sudden plague of crown-of-thorns appeared in the Red Sea and just as suddenly disappeared. Investigation disclosed that when the sea-star population reached a high concentration, fish that ordinarily ignored them began to eat them. As a result, many scientists have concluded that sudden epidemics of stars among the corals are natural cyclical phenomena that are best left alone lest the delicate ecological balance of the reef be upset.

More variegated than the sea stars but less often seen because they are smaller and more retiring are the brittle stars, which take their name from their disconcerting mode of defense. When attacked, a brittle star distracts its predator by jettisoning one of its five arms, often breaking it into several pieces while it makes a hasty retreat to regrow the missing appendage.

The most spectacular brittle star is the basket star. Each of its five arms branches into two armlets, which in turn branch again and again until the creature's outer edge is a maze of snaky tendrils. By day, basket stars pass for a tangled heap of dead gorgonian corals. But at night they stand on the tips of their arms, forming an inverted basket covered with a fine net of grasping tendrils ready to snare any small creature that passes through.

African red sea star

A Reef Galaxy

The most striking characteristic of a sea star is its set of radial arms. These may be as blunt and as relatively stiff as the wedge-shaped points of the giant yellow star (below) or as slender and flexible as the tubular arms of the red finger star (opposite, top). Some stars can perform dexterous tricks with their arms, such as turning a slow-motion somersault to right themselves when they have been turned upside down. Also, a sea star is capable of walking with its arms, even though they are not true limbs, adapted for such purposes as in most animals. Each arm contains a branch of the sea star's digestive and reproductive organs and, out near the tip, a rudimentary eye.

However, the long tendril-like arms of the sea star's cousin, the brittle star, shown here emerging from its daytime hiding place in a vase sponge (opposite, bottom), are real limbs. The brittle star uses them not only to move about the rocky coral flats but also to capture minute worms and mollusks. Brittle stars are among the most graceful of reef dwellers. At night, when they gather to scavenge, large groups move across the reef like submerged fishing fleets, casting their many-tendriled arms like nets.

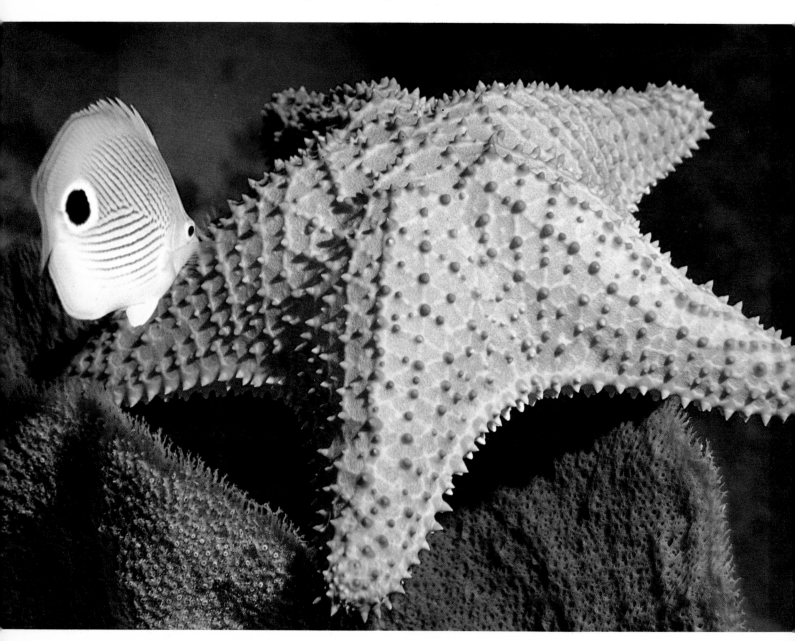

45

Stellar Feasting

Through its ability to regenerate limbs lost in the frays of reef competition, the predatory sea star has an insurance policy when it is preyed upon itself. In the two pictures on this page, the crown-of-thorns sea star, notorious for its reef destruction, clings to the bone-white skeleton of coral that it has completely denuded of living polyps. In the close-up at left, the tiny suction cups that line the creature's arms can also be seen. Other stars use these cups to pry open the shells of bivalves, but the crown-of-thorns employs them primarily for moving around and holding onto the coral while it eats.

The sea star itself may provide a morsel for a gaudy harlequin shrimp when it loses a limb in battle (opposite). Here, the shrimp is having a second helping—from an amputated arm of a sea star—although it would never attack the original owner.

Crustaceans

If the flamboyant tropical fish are the beauties of the world of the reef, the crustaceans are the grotesques. Members of the class Crustacea range in size from the smallest krill, the principal food of many whales, to lobsters that weigh up to 34 pounds. The visible characteristics all crustaceans have in common are double sets of antennae, multiple, jointed legs and horny external skeletons that may be as thin as paper or tough enough to provide a serviceable suit of armor. Some, like the lobsters, swim backward; others, such as crabs, mostly swim and walk sidewise; and barnacles spend solitary adult lives isolated and immobile in permanently anchored, stony cones. Still others have swiveled eyeballs set on the ends of stalks. Many are equipped with clumsy-looking pincers, which they wield with the expertise of fencers.

Seafood fanciers have elevated three of the crustacean clan—lobsters, crabs and shrimps—to such heights of gastronomic eminence that most of the 26,000 other crustaceans are virtually unknown. Lobsters of the frigid waters of the North Atlantic are the most highly prized for the flesh of their ungainly claws and tails, but the warm reef waters of the world are the homes of several breeds, such as the South Atlantic lobsters and crayfish, which are the mainstays of frozen-food industries. Unlike their northern cousins, reef lobsters are usually clawless, but their whip-like antennae are effective weapons that they use to lash at predators and strike down prey.

Lobsters, both the northern and tropical varieties, have some peculiar characteristics that they share with shrimps and crabs. As they grow, they must shed their exterior skeletons and grow larger-sized shells. They are extremely vulnerable without their armor and must go into hiding to avoid their enemies until they grow replacement shells.

The seas are filled with creatures that prey on crustaceans, particularly baby lobsters. To insure continuation of the species a female lobster lays thousands of eggs, carrying them glued to her abdomen until they hatch. A lobster usually produces from 8,000 to 30,000 eggs. For their part, lobsters and crabs are as voracious as the enemies that prey on them and will eat almost anything they can get their claws on, living or dead, large or small, including their own young. Fortunately for their survival, lobster hatchlings are quickly scattered by underwater currents so that their cannibalistic parents cannot get at them; otherwise lobsters would be in danger of literally eating themselves into extinction. With their insatiable appetites, however, the scavenging lobsters, together with shrimps, are among the most efficient housekeepers of the reef, keeping its waters clean and free of animal and plant debris.

There are more than a thousand different kinds of crabs, most of them curious, comical-looking creatures with popping eyes and startled, resentful expressions. Those that dwell in the reef environment include several of the most interesting of all the crustaceans. The fiddler crab, like many reef animals, is a motley of colors. The male of the species has one huge claw that he moves back and forth the way a string player wields the bow of his violin. The claw is used for grasping prey, defense and attracting females. The tropical boxer crab defends itself in a manner that goes beyond the pugilistic image in its name: It tears stinging tentacles from sea anemones and brandishes them in both claws at would-be predators. The blue crab, which is found from the cold waters of New England to the tropical reefs off the east coast of Mexico, swims with a side stroke, crooking the elbow of one claw so that it cuts through the water like a ship's prow. With legs that extend laterally from their oval bodies, nearly all crabs characteristically run sideways instead of forward along the sandy bottoms and beaches.

The most adaptable member of the crab family is the hermit crab (*Petrochirus diogenes*), which, because it has no shell of its own, must spend much of its life house hunting. Newborn, it immediately seeks and backs into any small abandoned snail shell in the vicinity. As it grows, the young hermit must repeatedly find new shells into which it can fit as its body outgrows each borrowed casing. To do this it scurries around the beach and tidal shallows, wriggling rear end first into random shells in the vicinity until it finds the right size and looking for all the world, according to one writer, "like a woman shopping for a girdle."

Shrimps live together in large groups on the sea floor. Lacking heavy armor and effective claws, they must depend on flight for protection against dozens of creatures that prey on them. Their fast swimming ability and prolific reproduction help offset the attrition: Females lay from 300,000 to 400,000 eggs at a time. Many exotic varieties of shrimps live in the tropical reefs, including at least two that are called coral shrimp: the banded coral shrimp, a thin, delicately striped creature that is a favorite of aquarium keepers, and the golden coral shrimp, which lives directly on coral branches.

Arrow crab

Kings of the Reef

Lobsters are one of the largest of the crustaceans and, by extension, of the phylum Arthropoda, which includes 90 percent of all the creatures (mostly insects) of the earth. They are also the most highly esteemed of all seafood, sought after so eagerly that in 1963 France and Brazil came to the verge of naval warfare over the right to fish for spiny lobsters off the coast of South America (the matter was settled amicably by negotiation after a French destroyer was dispatched to the scene).

Though the ferocious-looking lobsters of the North Atlantic, with their ungainly but succulent claws, are the expensive perquisites of epicures, even more valuable commercially are the clawless lobsters of the tropical reefs, whose edible parts are exported all over the world as rock lobster tails. The commonest of these, *Panulirus argus* (opposite)—known variously as spiny lobster, West Indian lobster, *langosta*, Florida lobster or southern crayfish—is an inhabitant of coral reefs in the tropical Atlantic. (*Panulirus guttatus*, the rock lobster, is a white-freckled cousin that shares the spiny lobster's habitat and its fate as a frozen-food delicacy.) The regal slipper lobster (below) inhabits reefs and atolls of the Pacific and has tiny, frail antennae, unlike those of all other lobsters, which it hides under horny, blinkerlike flaps.

Each autumn male and female lobsters of the American tropics leave the shelter of their reefs and assemble for a peculiar trek to their annual meeting grounds. In undulating conga lines of hundreds of members they walk head to tail, in single files along the ocean floor for 60-odd miles to the deep waters to new food sources and to mate.

Like grotesque monsters out of a science-fiction tale, two spiny lobsters (below) meet in the shelter of a Bahamian reef, using their knobby but sensitive antennae as sensors. The multicolored slipper lobster on the opposite page, which vaguely resembles a jeweled dancing shoe, is completely at home among the pink anemones of its retreat in a Hawaiian reef.

Shell Shacks

Because their bodies are long and cylindrical rather than round and flattened, hermit crabs are classified separately from other crabs. These crabs seek shelter within empty shells (above and opposite) to protect their soft and defenseless abdomens. Their hermitages are usually the coverings that once belonged to such gastropods as whelks and periwinkles. If a mollusk is still residing in the shell on which a crab has its eye, the hermit may or may not dispossess and devour it, depending on the size of the resident mollusk. But if another, smaller hermit is found within a shell, a battle for ownership always ensues.

Hermit crabs often share their shells' exteriors with other animals, such as sea anemones (left). While the anemone offers protection and perhaps even camouflage for the hermit, the crab provides transportation to richer feeding grounds for the otherwise stationary animal.

From Queensland to the Great Barrier Reef

by Noel Monkman

The pellucid waters and brilliant tropical sunshine surrounding Australia's Great Barrier Reef provide an ideal environment for the flourishing marine life there and some breathtaking scenery for the camera's lens. Noel Monkman, an Australian underwater photographer, set up a base camp in one of the small islands in the midst of the enormous reef and began to record on film and in prose the teeming life he encountered. He was especially taken with the activities and antics of the hermit crab. A seemingly passive, ill-tempered loner, the hermit turned out to be an aggressive fighter, a determined house hunter and a passionate, if neglectful, lover. The passage below describes a brief period in the life of a hermit crab.

Apart from eating, loving, and fighting, the main occupation of the hermit-crab is house-hunting, for as it grows the sitting-room in its shell becomes cramped, and so every shell it encounters in its wanderings is looked upon as a potential home. It matters not how worn and dilapidated the shell may be, it is always given a thorough examination with a view to occupation. Perhaps the new shell is too small—perhaps only half the size of the one the hermit-crab already possesses. Even so, it is turned this way and that, claws are inserted in the shell, and perhaps it is even given a try-out as a residence. This movement from one shell to the other must be carefully observed, for it is done so speedily that the details may easily be missed. It would seem that the creature is always aware of the danger of exposing its soft body to attack by a reef inhabitant. To make the change over the crab carefully places the new shell in position with its opening facing it; it grips the edge of the new shell with its claws, then in a flash withdraws its body from the old home and slips its tail into the new. The hermit-crab now attempts to back completely into the shell until nothing can be seen but its heavily armoured claws barring the doorway. If the new shell happens to be too small, the crab cannot back far enough into it, and after a few ineffectual attempts to ram itself deeper into the shell, it whips back into its previous home.

But while all this has been going on, another hermit-crab in search of a new home has appeared on the scene. The newcomer immediately attacks, and our hermit-crab wheels valiantly to meet the unprovoked attack. With their big claws extended, the combatants clash together; it is all-in fighting, with no holds barred. Backwards and forwards rages the battle, as each furiously attempts to pull its opponent from its shell. Fortunately, apart from the tender hind part, hermit-crabs are as heavily armoured as any crab. Here is a point to ponder upon in watching this miniature battle. Many a time I have attempted to drag a hermit-crab from its shell; it will part with its limbs (it will later grow new ones), but it will not relinquish its hold upon the shell. If one exerts too much force, the hermit-crab will be torn in half rather than allow its tender body to be withdrawn from the shell. And yet it is obvious that each of the contestants is attempting to do this very thing to its opponent. For its size, the hermit-crab is very powerful, and can support nearly thirty times the weight of its own body by the grip of one claw. We humans, unless trained athletes, can seldom support more than two-thirds of the weight of our bodies with the grip of the right hand.) The pull of the crab on its opponent is nothing as compared to the force a human hand can exert when attempting to drag a hermit-crab from its shell: no hermit-

crab's strength is sufficient to tear its opponent in half. How then can either warrior expect to vanquish his foe?

The explanation is that the hermit-crabs use the tactics of "nerve warfare". Each crab relies upon the fury and bluster of its attack to bluff its opponent into surrender, and the warrior of faint-heart is beaten before the fight really begins. Since the whole point of the attack is to pull the other fellow out, the only token of surrender is for the loser to loosen the powerful tail grip, and allow the victor crab to pull him out. A strange thing about these fights is that once the vanquished crab is out of its shell the victor never seems to follow up its advantage by attacking its unarmoured and dangerously exposed opponent. The vanquished hermit-crab scuttles away, but only to the nearest cranny in which it can hide its soft body. The victor never pursues, but centres its whole attention upon the now empty shell. Reaching inside with its big claw, it reconnoitres the roominess of the apartment. Satisfied with this, it then turns the shell about, examining it from all angles. Instinct seems to have gone all astray here, for the shell it already occupies may be a handsome one, and certainly a more suitable size for the proportions of its owner; whereas the shell of the vanquished is perhaps a battered specimen liberally bespattered with limy incrustations and empty worm tubes. However, a change of abode is soon made and, leaving its previous pleasant home behind, the victor departs with its tail firmly tucked into its tumbledown shack. It has hardly left the scene before the loser in the battle scuttles out of the cavity where it has been sheltering and swiftly takes possession of the handsome new house lately vacated by the winner of the fight.

Peering out from this new home, he sights a small hermit-crab wandering across the bottom of the pool. With a sudden rush he is across the sand, but not before the smaller crab has had a chance to withdraw into its shell. He rolls the other shell over and feels inside, but the small crab has withdrawn far back into the shell, and his large claw cannot force its way into the doorway. Straddling the shell he waits. What a bully! Does he wish to forget his late defeat by a victory over this small opponent? This crab is only a third his size, and if he drags it from its shell he will never fit his bulky body into a house so small. But this, dear reader, is love: the dainty little shell holds a female hermit-crab!

As I have said, one of the ruling passions of the hermit-crab is love, and his methods are those of the caveman. Coyly the female peers out from her shell. Immediately he makes a quick grab for her, whereupon she withdraws into her shell beyond his reach. Apparently even amongst crabs it is not ladylike to appear too willing. Impatiently her lover waits outside her doorway, but not for long, for within a minute or two her long antennae emerge, followed by two eyes on the end of their long stalks, and she surveys her lover. Perhaps pleased with his appearance, she emerges a little further, and in a flash he has grabbed one of her hind-legs and hangs on. At first she tries desperately to get back into her shell, but he ignores her vain struggles and strolls off, dragging her after him by the hind-leg. He may be a boorish lover, but at least he attends to the details of the wedding breakfast, for as he strolls along he pauses now and again to scratch up particles of food, which she accepts as they drift her way. After an hour or so of strolling and feeding in this fashion, he would appear to consider that the honeymoon is proceeding rather slowly, for he now turns round, grips her, and with a sudden jerk lifts her almost free of her shell, and they embrace. This embrace ensures another generation of hermit-crabs.

It is a brief love-making, and although the lady now seems willing to accept his attentions, never does he relinquish his grip on her hind-leg, but continues to stroll about, dragging her willynilly with him. Every hour or so he remembers her, but only long enough for another short embrace. Rounding a clump of coral, he is suddenly attacked by another hermit-crab, who, with a furious buffet, sends him rolling back across the sand. His wife has been flung some distance away, but she quickly rights herself, and calmly commences to pick up small particles of food from the sand, daintily transferring these to her mouth as she watches her husband do battle. The issue is not long in doubt, for with a sudden jerk, the newcomer drags her husband from his shell and casts him to the sand. With a desperate rush, he attempts to regain his shell, but another furious blow sends him tumbling. Taking no further notice of him, the newcomer strolls across to the lady, who is placidly feeding. Within a minute or two he has clasped her dainty hind-leg, and as the former husband regains possession of his shell his wife is accepting the attentions of her new lover.

Usually the fights between hermit-crabs are of short duration. Either one or the other speedily decides it has met its match, and lets itself be drawn from its shell, so concluding the duel. But I once filmed a fight between two hermit-crabs that lasted, off and on, for three days. One crab was slightly smaller than the other, but it would not succumb to the usual war of nerves, and clung tenaciously to its shell. Not even when its larger opponent pulled the claws from the smaller crab's body would it give in, and when it had no further weapons with which to carry on the fight, it withdrew deep within its shell. The victor, evidently considering that the honours of war were his, left his shell and rammed his own body in on top of all that was left of the smaller hermit-crab. This is the only instance I have seen of what appeared to be a fight to the death. It would appear that nearly all hermit-crab fights are a matter of bluffing the other fellow out of his shell.

For sheer entertainment, I can recommend a day watching hermit-crabs.

Crab Strategy

The true crabs are the most highly developed of all the crustaceans. Two of the more interesting species are the fiddler crab (below) and the spider crab (right). While female fiddlers have two normal-sized feeding pincers, the males have one immensely enlarged claw (the "fiddle"), which they wave about in distinctive patterns in order to attract females and indicate their readiness to mate. These enormous appendages also serve effectively as defensive weapons capable of inflicting serious wounds. And the fiddler doesn't stop there. Once the crab has a firm grasp on its foe it often casts off the entire arm, which remains attached to the attacker, and scurries to safety. Later, the fiddler grows a normal-sized claw in place of the one shed, while its undamaged claw grows to "fiddle" proportions.

Although the spider crab's defensive behavior is more passive than the fiddler's, it is usually as effective. The spider's carapace is studded with stiff hairs and spines to which it pinions such camouflage as algae, hydroids or seaweed. Some spider crabs have so many growths plastered to their bodies that they easily deceive even the sharpest-eyed potential enemies.

Clean-up Detail

Along with lobsters, crayfish and crabs, shrimps belong to the order Decapoda, the name referring to the 10 jointed legs identifying these crustaceans. Several pairs are used to handle food, while others serve primarily as a means of locomotion. Still others are used in reproduction—by the males to transfer sperm to the females and by the females to cradle packets of eggs until they are ready to hatch.

Many species of shrimps live among the world's reefs and have evolved special behavioral adaptations to their coral environment. Some have formed symbiotic relation-ships with other reef dwellers, such as sea anemones (over-leaf) and fish. Among these are the so-called cleaner shrimps. They include the banded coral shrimp (below) and the golden shrimp (opposite). Waving their long white antennae, they attract the attention of reef fish such as the angelfish, which gather around the cleaner shrimp and placidly wait to be relieved of the parasites and bacteria that often plague them. When the shrimps have had their fill, they abruptly cease their services, forcing the un-groomed fish to move on to other cleaning stations.

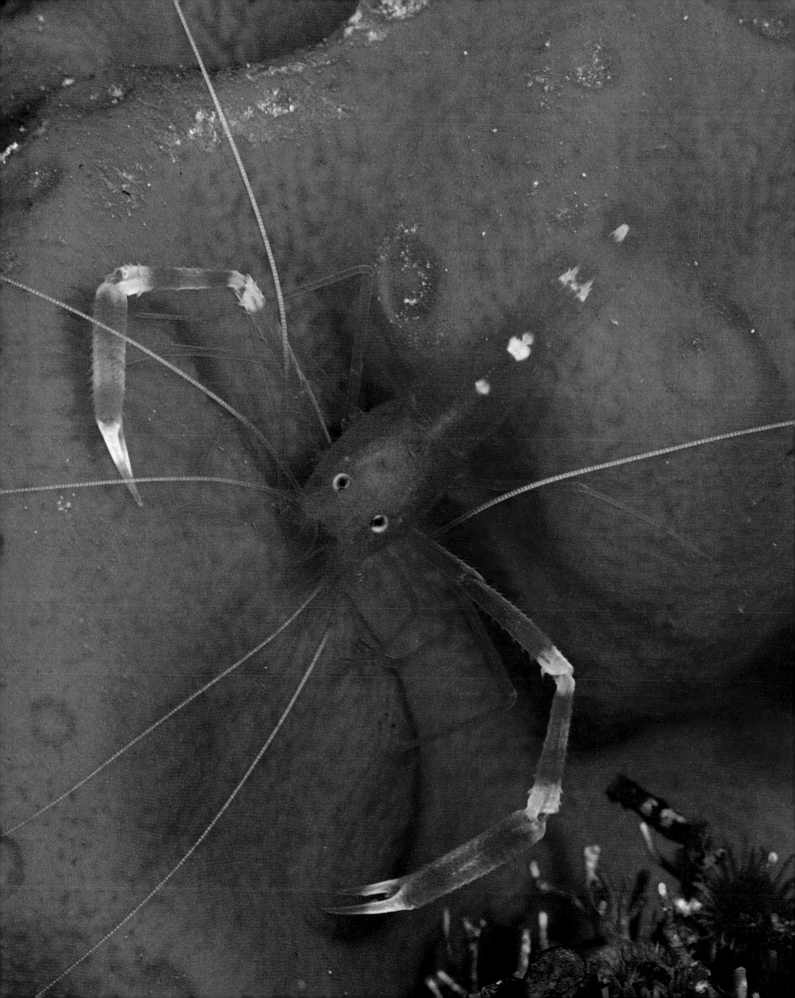

The anemone crab (below) and the anemone shrimp (opposite) are two extravagantly colored crustaceans that can afford to attract attention to themselves. Both live securely among the stinging tentacles of sea anemones, which protect them from predatory fish without harming the crustaceans themselves. From their snug base the crab and shrimp scavenge scraps discarded by fish and leftovers from the anemones.

Sea Urchins

The warm, shallow tidal pools between reef and shore shelter many relatives of the sea stars, although they seem to bear little family resemblance to their kin. Among the most conspicuous of these so-called echinoderms are the sea urchins—especially the hatpin urchin, which bristles like an oversized pincushion with dozens of needlelike spines, often a foot long, sticking out of a small spherical shell. Of all the echinoderms, it is the most deserving of the name, which comes from the Greek word *echinos*, spiny, and the Latin word *derma*, skin. Alone or in clusters of twos and threes, hatpin urchins make their bristly appearance nearly everywhere around the reef at night. They perch atop rocks or clumps of coral, lie openly on a sandy bottom, or hide in the meadows of turtle grass, where they graze on algae and plant debris, their principal foods.

The hatpin urchins appear in greatest numbers, however, at the base of the reef wall. During the day many wriggle into small depressions with their spines exposed, so that a diver sees nothing but a thicket of dark quills. If he swims too close, the spines stir into motion, swiveling in ball-and-socket joints on the urchins' shells to follow the movements of any potential molester. The experienced reef explorer learns to give them a wide berth, for short of a stray shark or barracuda, they are as dangerous as any creature he is likely to encounter in coral waters. Sea urchins' fragile, barbed spines are coated with a noxious mucus, and the spines break at the slightest touch and become embedded in the skin, causing an immediate stinging pain and, later, inflammation.

With such formidable protection, the hatpin urchin enjoys relative immunity from attack, as do a host of smaller creatures that make their home, unharmed, amid the poisonous spines. Most notable are the tiny shrimpfish, which do a headstand so that their black stripes blend with the urchins' quills, and the cardinal fish that live among the stinging spines. A larger fish, however, has found a clever way to get around the prickly defense to prey on the urchin. The triggerfish blows strong jets of water at the urchin, eventually rolling it over on its back and exposing its defenseless underside, which it proceeds to devour.

Not all sea urchins of the coral flats have such formidable armaments as the hatpin, but most are well protected. The short-spined urchins that abound in the dark patches of turtle grass can be safely handled, but they camouflage themselves with strands of seaweed and bits of coral among their spines. Closer to shore, the black rock-boring urchin protects itself against predators and pounding waves by jamming itself against the sides of its hole, using its short, stout spines like girders.

Another group of very different-looking echinoderms, the sea cucumbers, shares the rocky and sandy bottoms of the reef with the sea urchins. Looking more like large fat worms with leathery skin than raw material for a tossed salad, sea cucumbers are easy to spot against the pristine coral sands. They vary in length from three inches to four feet and substitute cylindrical symmetry for the radial silhouettes characteristic of other members of their phylum. At either end of their sausage-shaped bodies there is an opening; but when they are lying still, it is very difficult to make heads or tails of them. Only when a sea cucumber is feeding can its mouth be readily recognized by the moving mustache of branched tentacles surrounding it. Scavenging plankton and organic waste from the sea bed, most sea cucumbers use their tentacles to shove sand into their mouths. But some use the sticky appendages to pick up individual food particles daintily from the sand and then put them into their mouths like a child licking jam off his fingers. Most of the time a sea cucumber's posterior opening appears to be constantly active. As its body contracts and expands, a stream of water constantly renewed through its mouth carries the residue of the cucumber's sandy diet out. The contractions and dilations also indicate that the strange creature is breathing—through respiratory tubes located near its rear end. As the cucumber breathes, a long transparent fish may suddenly dart out of the opening. This is the pearlfish, which makes its home in the cloacal cavity at the lower end of the intestine of the cucumber and serves a symbiotic purpose that has not yet been discovered.

As they ripple slowly and ponderously across the coral flats, sea cucumbers may seem like sluggish creatures that mind their own business and are of little consequence to the life of the reef. But they play a very important role as housekeepers that thoroughly cleanse the sands of organic debris. The estimated 2,000 cucumbers living in a single acre of reef process up to 60 tons of sand a year, and at one time or another nearly every grain of the coral sands in their area will pass through their bodies.

In a shot that backfired, the black sea cucumber (opposite) is itself enmeshed in the sticky threads that it squirts out at would-be molesters. The yellow sea cucumber (below), instead of burrowing and consuming sand like most of its fellow cucumbers, perches upright and filters food from the water with the branching tentacles around its mouth.

Marine Cucumbers

For millions of years sea cucumbers have pursued a languid way of life on the coral bottoms with relative ease and safety because they have few natural enemies among the other reef creatures. Occasionally the pincer of a prying crab will provoke one of the sausage-shaped animals into protecting itself by shooting out a spray of viscous strands, a primitive defense netting shown covering the cucumber at left. Only rarely does the situation become serious enough for some cucumbers to resort to the ultimate defense of ejecting their viscera to distract the attacker.

In the last few hundred years, however, a serious threat to the sea cucumber has come from a predator that lives outside the reef: man. As untempting as these lumpish sea cucumbers may seem to the Western palate, they are considered a great delicacy and even an aphrodisiac throughout much of the Orient, where they are known as trepang. Chinese chefs especially delight in pleasing gourmets by concocting a soup with tidbits of smoked trepang as the main ingredient. As a result, hundreds of tons of sea cucumbers are fished out of the waters of the Great Barrier Reef each year and shipped to Hong Kong to meet the demand, and the sea cucumber becomes increasingly rare.

The Ocean Island
by Gilbert Klingel

To adopt a private island, to know a faraway place and its inhabitants so well that it can be called home, is a wistful dream that many people have but few manage to fulfill. Gilbert Klingel, an amateur naturalist, realized such a dream when he settled in Inagua, a small coral island in the Caribbean, and recorded his experiences in The Ocean Island. *In the passage below, his observations of the lowly sea urchin show that supposedly brainless creature in a new light.*

Centipedes are noted for the amazing number of their feet. But they are amateurs in the art of pedal dexterity compared with the sea urchins. Sea urchins are the porcupines of marine life; only a person with cast iron fingers would dare pick one up, for every inch of their bodies is protected with long pointed spines which are mounted in cleverly designed ball and socket joints. They lived by the pool and along the cliff in great scattered masses, giving the rocks the appearance of being festooned with giant cockleburs. To fall on one would be a painful and dangerous experience, for their spines are frequently very poisonous, being covered with germ-filled mucus that produces festering wounds difficult to sterilize. Often the spines are barbed and very brittle, breaking off where they enter the flesh. One such injury in the fleshy part of my leg gave me no end of trouble until I dissected it out with a scalpel; even then it required more than a week to heal. The under sides of their barbed and pointed bodies are literally a mass of feet, strange sucker-like affairs arranged in symmetrical rows radiating from the round centrally located mouth. By means of these they progress slowly from place to place, advancing by a series of wavy rhythms. These tube-feet are capable of considerable contraction and expansion and no matter how uneven the surface on which they rest, they have a firm grip on the ground at every point. Thus they are able to cope with the surf, staying firmly in place while the water bubbles and roars over them. Sea urchins are considered to be but stupid automatons, headless creatures without a thought or flicker of intelligence. This is literally true, for they are the original scatterbrains. The only

nervous system they enjoy is distributed in a series of ganglia in a circle about their spherical bodies. Thus the sea urchin functions because its ganglia are stimulated by its moving parts. One moving part generates activity in its neighbor; the animal is managed by its own activity. It might be said that the essential difference between an animal with a brain and one without, as for example, a dog and a sea urchin, lies in the fact that a dog moves the legs, in a sea urchin the legs move the animal. But be this as it may I could not help admiring the manner in which these living cockleburs had carved a niche for themselves in the face of terrific odds. Any animal that can survive in a world of crashing surf while managing several hundred separate feet at once, brainless or not, is a creature of no small attainments. Most of us have trouble enough at times managing two.

How very wonderful these sea urchins were I did not know until I had watched them for a long time from the sanctuary of my bath. One of the things that always astonished me was the immaculate appearance of their bodies. Although the surf at times piled loose carpets of torn seaweed over the boulders and cast up gritty piles of loose gravel and coarse sand, and although all the other animals, the snails, mussels and chitons, had a rubbed worn look, or were covered with parasitic barnacles, the sea urchins were always spotless; no grains of sand, strands of algae or blotches of parasites marred their jet black coats. This was particularly remarkable when one considered that their spines should have been catch-alls for all manner of debris. They had a very clever system of keeping themselves clean. When a fragment of sand or dirt fell between the needles, it was grasped by a tiny clamp or pincers equipped with a triple set of jaws, like those of certain types of dredges; these were mounted on a flexible shaft of muscle and skin which transported the debris to the next claw which carried it to another, or to one of the tube feet which were also scattered over portions of the creature's upper surface, and so on until the offending fragment was dropped into the water. Small parasites that slipped between the barrier of spines were not treated so gently. The moment they touched the urchin's side the claws began snapping, opening and shutting until they seized on some portion of the animal's anatomy. Once a pincers secured a grip it held on tenaciously and then if a struggle ensued, other claws came to its rescue until the captive was held rigid by myriad tiny clamps. Only death of the parasite caused the grip to be relaxed; the corpse was then passed from claw to claw, foot to foot until it reached the urchin's mouth and was devoured.

The hundreds of tube feet were not the only method these animal cacti utilized in retaining their position in life. Great numbers of them lived in cavities in the rocks; their bodies were larger than the entrances to their caves. These cave-dwelling individuals were about as safe as it is possible to be, for they were guarded by their spines and could not be approached from any direction except directly in front. They paid a penalty, however, for their security for they were hopeless prisoners. Early in life when they

had stationed themselves at some favorable spot they secreted a powerful corrosive which crumbled the soft coral rock beneath them. Soon they were well out of the way of the driving water, safe in their holes. But then as they grew it became necessary to expand their quarters; the acid and the surf etched away the walls until they fitted comfortably but the openings remained comparatively small. They reminded me of those human beings who spend a lifetime carving niches for themselves only to find that in the end they are completely enmeshed by the fruits and habits of their ambitions. All about the pool were dozens of these imprisoned urchins. They seemed as healthy and as fully formed as their freer relatives. The free individuals, however, probably found food more abundant, for they lived on seaweed and algae which they ground up in their peculiar five-sided jaws; the prisoners had to be content with whatever the passing waters brought them—the inner surfaces of their dens were eaten quite clean and barren.

Pincushions

About all that can be seen of a sea urchin are its formidable defenses—its tough shell surmounted by spines that vary in form from the long needles of the hatpin urchin (below) to the shorter bristles of the blue urchin (left) to the blunt clubs of the scarlet slate pencil urchin (opposite). Only the animals shown overleaf and a few other urchin-eaters are able to penetrate this briar-patch armament.

Located inside the mouth on the underside of the urchin is one of the most remarkable organs in the animal kingdom. Called Aristotle's lantern because the Greek philosopher described it in the fourth century B.C. as looking like an oil lamp of the period, it is a circle of five pie-shaped teeth controlled by 40 pieces of skeleton that operate somewhat like the jaws of a mechanical crane. This device is so versatile and powerful that it enables the urchin to pick up and chew a wide variety of plant or animal material, living or dead, and to gnaw burrows into hard coral.

A starfish (left) handles the touchy task of eating a sea urchin the same way that it consumes clams and oysters—by extruding the gauzy membrane of its stomach over the victim's exposed underside and then digesting it at leisure. Once in the grip of a sea star, an urchin is doomed, and its pincushion defenses cannot save it.

A triton snail devours a prickly meal of sea urchin in these two pictures (opposite, top). In the nearer view, the giant snail rears up to its full height as it extends its massive fleshy foot to begin enveloping the urchin. In the detail (far right), the triton's foot wraps tightly around the urchin as it attacks its prey with its rasplike tongue.

On a reef in the West Indies, a Spanish hogfish (opposite, bottom) nonchalantly chews a spiny morsel of a sea urchin that it has torn apart with its powerful jaws. Nearby, another curious fish examines a discarded piece of the unfortunate echinoderm, keeping a respectful distance from the formidable hogfish.

Sponges and Worms

The nutrient-rich waters of the reef encourage the proliferation of many simple animals—notably sponges, bryozoa and worms. Like the anemones and the corals, most of these primitive creatures are easily mistaken for the plants in the lush underwater gardens.

Only a rung up the evolutionary ladder from the most primitive one-celled animals (such as plankton) are sponges, which are little more than colonies of cells living together to extract food efficiently from the seawater. Some sponges live on the slopes of the reef and deep in the dark coral caves. These sponges spread out into flat velvety encrustations—garish patchwork carpets of yellow, green, purple and red. Sponges, however, can sprout upward in a fanciful and seemingly endless variety of shapes: fans and fingers, cushions and chalices, vases and other vessels. Barrel sponges that live near the edge of the North American continental slope reach a height of approximately five feet and have a nearly equivalent diameter.

These varieties supply the familiar commercial sponge, which is only the skeleton of the animal. When the sponge is alive, the framework is covered with a thin gelatinous skin, and the surface is perforated with thousands of invisible microscopic holes, or pores, which take in water. The visible holes expel water after food has been strained out and digested. Apart from this filtration system, sponges have no specialized organs. But each cell as an individual performs a special function, grabbing food particles from the passing current, or sending out sperm and eggs for reproduction, or building the skeleton. The most highly specialized are the cylindrical cells lining the hundreds of channels in a sponge's body, which digest food and eject waste. Each such cell has a tiny whip, and the incessant beating of these filaments enables a sponge to filter water up to a thousand times its own bulk in an hour.

Spread widely throughout the leeward side of the reef are other simple, colony-dwelling animals—the minute and inconspicuous bryozoa, or moss animals, so named because they often form small mosslike tufts. Polyplike creatures that bear a strong resemblance to coral, they are more advanced than either coral or sponges because each member of the colony is a distinct individual complete with tentacles, mouth, alimentary canal and primitive nervous system. The white brittle filigrees of bryozoa appear on the shady side of rocks and shells, and sometimes they hang like lacework spreads on the underside of seaweeds. Very often they mock plants, taking on erect, shrublike forms. In such structures the bryozoa live side by side in orderly compartments made of lime or a tough gelatinous fleshy material.

The numerous worms on the reef have a circulatory system and the beginnings of a brain and are somewhat more advanced than the other reef primitives. Yet many are curiously plantlike in appearance. The sedentary tube worms, which are among the most beautiful animals in the world, might easily be mistaken for tiny flowers on a head of brain coral when they extend their vivid feathery tentacles or gills to absorb oxygen and collect particles of food from the sea. Always covered with fine filaments and brilliantly colored, these gills have provided the various species of tube worms with some very descriptive common names: plume worms, with gills that twist upward in swirling concentric spirals; feather-duster worms, which hold theirs in upright clusters; and peacock worms, which spread their gills so that they look like inverted parasols.

Many other worms inhabit the reef. They live in much the same way as their distant cousin, the earthworm, by digging tunnels through the deep sands and dead coral and absorbing nutrients as the material passes through their bodies. One worm, however, is an active predator—the graceful, iridescent *Nereis*, which comes in many sizes and shapes, some growing as large as a half-foot long and an inch wide. *Nereis* and its nearest relatives are protected by hundreds of fine bristles and armed with powerful jaws which permit them to eat many small crustaceans, other worms and carrion.

A relative of this worm, the palolo, stages one of the reef's most spectacular annual events. Reclusive and intensely sensitive to light, palolos venture out of their burrows deep in the dead coral only at night. But as the spawning season approaches, the rear part of their bodies begins to fill with eggs or sperm. Then, on certain nights each year, the egg- or sperm-filled sections break off, and in the predawn, millions of these writhing and twisting members can be seen churning the surface of the water as they spill their sex cells. Off Samoa this spectacle always occurs annually during the last quarter of the moon in October or November and is celebrated by a great feast among the island natives, who consider the worm a delicacy.

Serpulid worms anchored in hard coral

The tubeworms' vanishing act is recorded in this sequence of pictures. Here, the tentacles of two plume worms are fully extended above their burrows.

Only a fraction of a second later the plume worms have drawn more than half of their spiraling flowery tentacles into the havens of their limy tubes.

The hasty retreat is almost complete; only the tip of the nearer plume worm is visible. It is already well protected by the sharp, thorny projection on the top of the tube.

Plumed Bonnets

Swirling crowns of plumate tentacles fluttering gently in the tropical undercurrent are all that can be seen here of the cluster of tubeworms above. The bodies and most of the heads of these spectacular undersea relatives of the homely earthworm are usually buried in the tubular refuges from which they take their name.

Although they are mobile when hatched, tubeworms quickly settle down to a stationary existence, fashioning a permanently fixed tube from which they never venture. Some burrow a hole into living coral and encase them-selves in it by secreting a chalky material. Others create an external tube on the surface of the reef by cementing to-gether bits of sand and shell with mucus. To insure com-plete privacy, many tubeworms have a spoon-shaped ap-pendage that they can use like a trap door to close the opening of their home, and the particles of debris that adhere to its sticky surface provide excellent camouflage. At the slightest disturbance the worm's feathery headdress vanishes instantly (opposite), and the opening cannot be distinguished from the surrounding terrain.

77

The Edge of the Sea

by Rachel Carson

The Atlantic palolo worms spend their lives hidden in the dead foundations of coral reefs, but once a year, under the spell of a July moon, the worms light up the sea in a phosphorescent spectacle when they spawn. Rachel Carson, the noted marine biologist and conservationist, witnessed such a "pyrotechnic display" one magic night in the Florida Keys and set down her impressions in the following excerpt from her classic study of the American coastline, The Edge of the Sea.

On certain nights of the year, extraordinary events occur over the reefs. The famed palolo worm of the South Pacific, moved to gather in its prodigious spawning swarms on a certain moon of a certain month—and then only—has its less-known counterpart in a related worm that lives in the reefs of the West Indies and at least locally in the Florida Keys. The spawning of this Atlantic palolo has been observed repeatedly about the Dry Tortugas reefs, at Cape Florida, and in several West Indian localities. At Tortugas it takes place always in July, usually when the moon reaches its third quarter, though less often on the first quarter. The worms never spawn on the new moon.

The palolo inhabits burrows in dead coral rock, sometimes appropriating the tunnelings of other creatures, sometimes excavating its burrow by biting away fragments of rock. The life of this strange little creature seems to be ruled by light. In its immaturity the palolo is repelled by light—by sunlight, by the light of the full moon, even by paler moonlight. Only in the darkest hours of the night, when this strong inhibition of the light rays is removed, does it venture from its burrow, creeping out a few inches in order to nibble at the vegetation on the rocks. Then, as the season for spawning approaches, remarkable changes take place within the bodies of the worms. With the maturing of the sex cells, the segments of the posterior third of each animal take on a new color, deep pink in the males, greenish gray in the females. Moreover, this part of the body, distended with eggs or sperm, becomes exceedingly thin walled and fragile, and a noticeable constriction develops between this and the anterior part of the worm.

At last there comes a night when these worms—so changed in their physical beings—respond in a new way to the light of the moon. No longer does the light repel and hold them prisoners within their burrows. Instead, it draws them out to the performance of a strange ritual. The worms back out of their burrows, thrusting out the swollen, thin-walled posterior ends, which immediately begin a series of twisting movements, writhing in spiral motions until suddenly the body breaks at the weak point and each worm becomes two. The two parts have different destinies—the one to remain behind in the burrow and resume the life of the timid forager of the dark hours, the other to swim up toward the surface of the sea, to become one of a vast swarm of thousands upon thousands of worms joining in the spawning activities of the species.

During the last hours of the night the number of swarming worms increases rapidly, and when dawn comes the sea over the reef is almost literally filled with them. When the first rays of the sun appear, the worms, strongly stimulated by the light, begin to twist and contract violently, their thin-walled bodies burst open, and the eggs from some and sperm from others are cast into the sea. The spent and empty worms may continue to swim weakly for a short time, preyed upon by fish that gather for a feast, but soon all that remain have sunk to the bottom and died. But floating at the surface of the sea are the fertilized eggs, drifting over areas many feet deep and acres in extent. Within them swift changes have begun—the division of cells, the differentiation of structure. By evening of that same day the eggs have yielded up tiny larvae, swimming with spiral motions through the sea. For about three days the larvae live at the surface; then they become burrowers in the reefs below until, a year hence, they will repeat the spawning behavior of their kind.

Some related worms that swarm periodically about the Keys and the West Indies are luminous, creating beautiful pyrotechnic displays on dark nights. Some people believe that the mysterious light reported by Columbus as seen by him on the night of October 11, "about four hours before making the landfall and an hour before moonrise," may have been a display of some of these "fireworms."

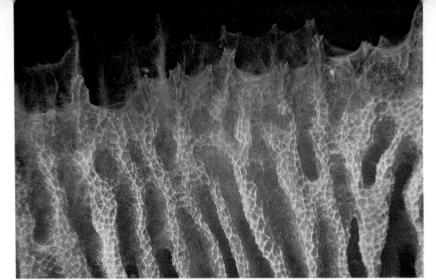

In this close-up view (left) of the upper edge of a vase sponge, a translucent coating covers its skeleton. The dried skeletal framework of many tropical sponges furnishes the absorbent material that appears in the bath and the kitchen. But some sponges have understructures of glassy silica, and others have chalky skeletons that are almost as hard as coral.

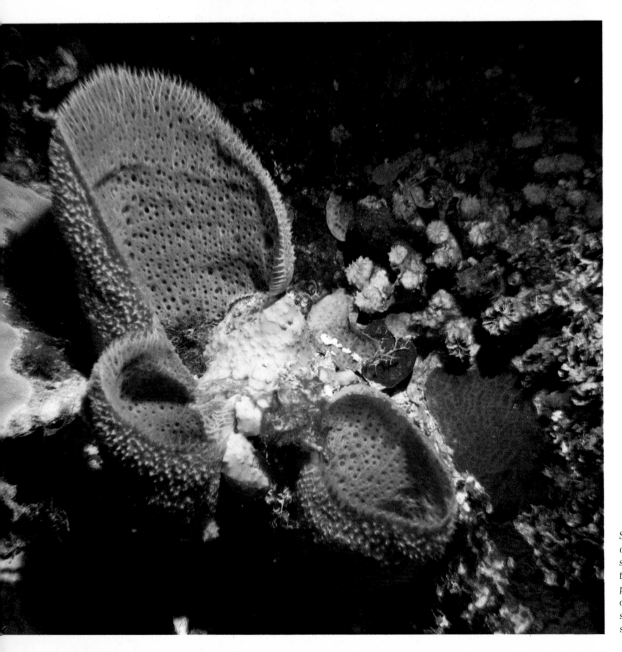

Sponges live both alone and in clusters. At left, three lavender vase sponges look like flower petals as they sprout out around a clump of peach-colored coral. On the opposite page, a luminous blue vase sponge displays itself in solitary splendor on the sea floor.

Filtration System

Firmly rooted in one spot for life, sponges look more like vegetation than any other reef dweller—especially when, like the ones shown here, their coloring is a delicate floral pastel. Aristotle was the first observer to point out that sponges are animals, but the absence of any digestive or nervous system led most later naturalists to believe that the ancient sage was mistaken. The sponge was dubbed not only an underwater relative of moss and fungus but also a unique combination of plant and animal life. Some scientists even believed that it was a nonliving substance secreted by the tiny crustaceans that make their homes in its pores. In 1765 naturalist John Ellis examined sponges closely and, observing them to be drawing water actively through their bodies and filtering it constantly for food, pronounced them animals once and for all, although it took another century to convince the doubters.

Sponges of the same species, differing widely in color despite their kinship, sometimes form colonies like the one shown at left. The variegated pattern consists of bits of orange and blue sponge growing on a yellow tube sponge.

On a reef off the Cayman Islands in the Caribbean, a cluster of sulphur-yellow tube sponges (below) thrusts upward like crooked chimneypots. In nearby waters a large red barrel sponge (opposite) attracts the attention of two brightly colored fish.

Mollusks

Long before wet suits and oxygen tanks enabled men to explore the varied wonders of the reef, many people visited the adjacent beaches and waded deep into the tidal pools in search of some of its most beautiful treasures—the shells of the many mollusks that live there.

In Australia, the aboriginal natives found the shell of one snail useful for scooping water from their boats and gave it the name bailer, while the Victorian colonists used the halves of the enormous giant clam for birdbaths. In the South Seas, islanders culled the piles of shells at the tide line to find the gleaming domed cowrie shells, which they traded as currency and wore in strings to enhance their own fertility.

Most reef mollusks inhabit the sheltered waters between the reef and the shore. Here the gastropods—snails and their close kin—abound in a vast assortment of sizes, from the gigantic horse conchs, which measure up to two feet, to the numerous minuscule snails less than a tenth of an inch long that can be found by the hundreds in a bucketful of coral sand. Among the more numerous of the visible small snails, which are also called univalves because of their single shell, are the neritas; their distinctive black-and-white-checked shells can be spotted everywhere in the tidal plains. Along the high water line and on the shore, the periwinkles—unusual water snails that are able to live out of water in moist areas for as long as a month at a time—are even more common. Many of the smaller snails are vegetarians that have found their niche in the food pyramid by eating what only a few other reef animals can—the hard crusts of microscopic algae that form on the pebbles, shells and dead coral. They get at their unusual diet with the aid of a rasplike tongue, called a radula, which is edged with scores of tiny teeth.

The monarchs of the snails, the knobby-shelled conchs, are omnivores that slide slowly through the turtle grass in search of carrion or red algae. But the conchs are exceptions, for most of the larger gastropods are carnivorous. Some, like the cowries, rasp away the flesh of stationary animals such as sponges, soft coral and anemones. Others—the cones, mitres, volutes, helmets and tritons—are active predators. Although slow-moving, most of these hunters are able to trap even more sedentary animals such as starfish and other gastropods and envelop them in the spreading folds of the fleshy part of their body, called a foot. The cone shells are able to catch much swifter prey,

including fish, although they are no faster than other snails. Armed with a magazine of small, highly toxic stingers, each attached to a long, slender thread, a cone shell harpoons its quarry, killing it almost instantly. Humans are just as susceptible to the cone shell's lethal darts as fish are. Several cases have been recorded of unsuspecting collectors who picked up the pretty striped shell only to be killed while they were admiring it.

Most gastropods are protected by their hard spiral shells and a trap door called an operculum that they can slam shut when they retreat inside. But there are some interesting exceptions. The gentle sea hares, whose tentacles sprout upright like a pair of rabbit ears, have only a residual shell, and their soft flesh covers it completely. For protection, sea hares rely on the camouflage of their sand-colored skins and on clouds of violet ink that they eject when disturbed. The spectacularly beautiful nudibranchs, or sea slugs, have no shell at all; they look like fantastically colored worms as they ripple sinuously over the tidal rocks.

The other mollusks that inhabit the coral zones along with the gastropods display an equally wide diversity. The primitive chiton, which has a shell with eight plates that looks like an armadillo's, uses its radula-tongue to scrape a hollow in hard rock and thereafter rarely travels more than a few feet from its nesting place even to feed. Another mollusk, the giant chambered nautilus, makes its flat spiraling shell by continually building new additions to its home while sealing off its old empty living quarters. The most unlikely-looking mollusks are the squids and octopuses, the most active of all invertebrates, which have a highly developed nervous system and no external shell. They can move rapidly enough to grab fish with the long flexible tentacles surrounding their mouths.

By far the largest group of mollusks that are not members of the snail clan are the twin-shelled bivalves—clams, oysters, mussels and scallops. In the graveyard of dead coral toppled and scattered by waves and tropical storms, great beds of these animals can be found with their shells opened to filter the plankton from the passing current. Many bivalves are completely stationary, anchored to their beds for life, and have only the most rudimentary eyes. But the scallops are a notable exception. They have dozens of bright-blue eyes lined up just inside the lips of their shells and can move through the water by flapping their shell halves together.

Flamingo tongue snail

The One That Got Away

When an adult sea star enfolds a bivalve in its deadly embrace there is virtually no escape, for oysters, clams and their kin are no match for the relentless power of the starfish's suction-cupped arms. Once the twin shells are pried open as much as a millimeter, the succulent creature inside is done for. Many bivalves are anchored together permanently in masses, unable to move, and when a star happens on a colony of them the result is often disaster, for the star will methodically reduce its prey to a pile of empty, gaping shells.

Happily for their family's survival, a few scallops and clams, notably the file clam shown on these pages, are mobile enough to escape the clutches of a star if they have sufficient warning. File clams, so called for their serrated, rasplike shells, have strong adductor muscles that open and close their shells and squirt water so that they are able to jet jerkily through the water in bounding movements that have earned them the name "jumping shells." They also have fringes of vermilion tendrils that frame their partly opened shells and serve as detectors of danger.

In the sequence at left a sea star, perched on a coral mound, stretches an arm toward an out-of-reach file clam just as the taste buds of the clam's sensitive tentacles inform it that an enemy is near. Clambering down, the star touches bottom at the moment the clam prepares to flee (center). In the bottom photograph, the bivalve bounds off to safety as the starfish makes a futile grasp at its lost meal.

Beady Blue Eyes of a Scallop

Venus was born of the sea full grown and sailed to earth in the bowl of a scallop shell, according to legend. And if the goddess has become the apotheosis of beauty, her fluted conveyance has become the most familiar of all shells, an artistic motif and an emblem of groups ranging from the medieval Crusaders to a modern oil company.

The interior of a present-day scallop shell is occupied by a strange-looking creature that only another mollusk could confuse with Venus. Unlike many bivalves, which stay firmly anchored to their beds after they reach maturity, scallops swim freely, if erratically, by jet propulsion, gulping in water and expelling it by means of a valvelike adductor muscle that opens and closes its half shells and propels it forward. As a limited aid to navigation, a scallop has dozens of beady blue eyes (opposite, enlarged nine and one half times). The double fringes of tentacles serve not only to filter passing plankton (as the Galápagos scallop, overleaf, is doing) but also as an organ of smell. Whenever the tentacles sense approaching danger, the scallop skitters off along the bottom, sending up a concealing cloud of sand or mud. Often scallops are accompanied by free-loading tunicates, translucent colonies of small creatures called sea squirts (below). In a commensal—meaning "eating together"—arrangement, the squirts attach themselves permanently to the bivalve's upper shell and share its movable feast of plankton.

Sea Shell Art Gallery

The beautiful shells of mollusks account for their widespread popularity and their consequent destruction by eager collectors. Often vivid and bizarre in color and form, shells are calcareous deposits secreted by the soft parts of the animal. They support and protect the soft flesh of the creature's body and are essential to the life of the mollusks that form them. Squids and nudibranchs (pages 96–97) have endured though their shells are respectively either so scanty or so covered with flesh that they provide no defense at all.

Favorite collector's items are the shells of the king conch, the New Caledonian chambered nautilus and the triton mollusk (opposite, top to bottom), as well as the lovely but often dangerous cone shells (left). All cone snails are fitted with sharp teeth that are connected to poison glands near the stomach. When a cone encounters a likely victim it slowly extends itself toward its prey. When the quarry is within reach, the cone suddenly injects the victim with a paralyzing venom. The poison of certain species is so potent that it has caused the deaths of several people who were unfortunate enough to step on them or pick them up.

Propped on its end for display, the handsome shell of the Conus amaralis would be a prized addition to any collection. Because of their reputation as killers, cones—a live specimen is shown above—are feared and avoided by inhabitants of their South Pacific habitat.

Extending its so-called foot over the side of its shell (left), a king conch slowly turns itself over. Denizens of the temperate waters of the South Atlantic Ocean and the Caribbean Sea, conchs are the largest of the gastropods and may weigh up to five pounds, with shells a foot long. The shells of conchs are highly prized as the material from which cameos are made, and their flesh makes a palatable chowder.

The gracefully curved shells at left belong to New Caledonian chambered nautiluses, immortalized in Oliver Wendell Holmes's poem "The Chambered Nautilus." The shells are partitioned into chambers, each of which is a former home of the nautilus, which sealed it off and added a new, more commodious cell as it grew bigger. The nautilus differs from other cephalopods in that it has between 80 and 90 tentacles, all of which lack the suction-cup tips that squids and octopuses use to hold their prey.

Similar to the king conch but with a slenderer shell that can grow to a length of 20 inches, the triton (left) is one of the largest gastropods. The triton inhabits Indo-Pacific waters, where it feeds primarily on bivalves and on echinoderms, notably the crown-of-thorns starfish. The triton is able to bypass the notorious starfish's spiny defenses and is the only known natural curb on that destroyer of coral reefs.

Mobile Mollusks

As their undulating tentacles propel their soft bodies briskly through the water, it is hard to believe that the octopus, squid and cuttlefish are close relatives of the sedentary clam and oyster, though all are mollusks. The cuttlefish (opposite) produces an internal shell made of the same limy substance from which the shells of clams and oysters are made.

The mobile mollusks belong to the class Cephalopoda, which means "head-footed." The name refers to the eight or more tentacles that spring from their heads and are used in seizing prey such as crabs and crayfish. The 10-armed cuttlefish in turn is preyed upon by such marine animals as small sharks and rays as well as by humans who sell its

internal shell or cuttlebone commercially to bird owners for their pets to sharpen their beaks on and its inky discharge to artists to make sepia pigment.

The octopus's commercial value is in its flesh, which is esteemed by food lovers all over the world. Although they have been maligned in literature and art, these solitary creatures are actually shy and retiring and pose little danger to man. The only known exception is the smallest of the family, the blue-ringed octopus (above). No larger than the palm of a man's hand, the four-inch blue-ring packs a venom so toxic that its mere presence in the water is enough to kill its crustacean prey. Several human fatalities have also resulted from the bite of this little rock dweller.

A brilliant "Spanish dancer" nudibranch glides across the ocean floor (left, top) in shallow water off Hawaii. The science-fiction dragon with a transparent body and rust-colored dorsal gills (left, center) is the sea slug, Hermissenda erassicornis. At left, bottom, two pelagic nudibranchs meet in a swirling mating rite.

The Philippine navy-blue nudibranch above is one of more than a thousand species of sea slugs distributed over the world's oceans. Opposite are two sea slugs common to the waters of Australia. When discovered at low tide clinging to rocks, or when disturbed, nudibranchs appear as colorless blobs, but in the calm of their underwater world they flower into unbelievable tints—more varied and brilliant than any other form of submarine animal life.

Slugfest

Nudibranchs are among the oddest of ocean creatures. Classified as mollusks, they have neither shell nor mantle. And their gills, when they are present at all (some genera have none and breathe through their skin), are not on their sides, where they appear in most aquatic animals. Their gills have developed into elaborate, plumelike "antlers" that stand along the creature's back and give the order its name, which means "exposed gills." Fancifully colored and wormlike in appearance, nudibranchs are commonly known as sea slugs, after their garden-pest cousins, the land slugs. Nudibranchs live in tidal pools and on the pilings of old docks. Born defenseless, some nudibranchs are able to consume poisonous anemones without harming themselves and retain the toxins for their own protection.

Fish

The limpid waters of coral reefs are the biggest, most densely populated fish tanks in the world. No other marine habitat supports such a diversity of fish in such numbers. In one area of Australia's Great Barrier Reef about 2,000 distinct species have been recorded. By contrast, the entire 1,200-mile seaboard of California, where practically no reefs occur, is home to only an estimated 350 species of inshore fish.

Equally impressive are the varied kinds of fish that crowd into extremely small areas of reef-girt waters. Ichthyologist C. Lavett Smith of the American Museum of Natural History has reported 70 to 80 species in the waters of a single reef section three yards in diameter in the Bahamas. The coexistence of so many varied species of fish in the same area is a phenomenon that occurs in no other marine environment. It poses a question about the basic, biological principle of competitive exclusion by which different species with similar ecological requirements tend to drive each other out of commonly occupied localities. In the case of reef fish, it is probably because the coral environment provides such abundant food that it easily supports many species.

Marine biologists speculate about the reasons for certain peculiarities that seem to be common denominators among most reef fish and set them apart from most others: brilliancy of hue, irregularity of markings and oddness of shape. As the biologists see it, these conspicuous colors and attention-calling stripes or spots may actually serve as a kind of social attraction or camouflage in the refracted underwater light that bathes tropical reefs. Vertical bars, horizontal stripes and bizarre splotches of color blur the recognizable contours of a fish and make it more difficult to see against the complex coral background than in front of a level seascape.

A good example of this camouflage principle is the Nassau grouper, which is striped like a convict and is commonly found in places where soft corals called sea whips are arrayed in vertical lines on the reefs. With its conspicuous striping, the grouper blends effectively with the sea whips around it. Another hider among the sea whips is the trumpetfish (*Aulostomus maculatus*), which has the advantage of being thin enough to imitate a sea whip.

Odd shape and coloration are also the defenses of the imperial angelfish (*Pomacanthus imperator*), with blue, black, yellow and green markings and a form so vague that it might be anything but a fish. Another skilled fool-the-eye artist is the butterflyfish, which camouflages its eyes with a masklike black band and often sports false "eyes" on both sides near its tail.

The undisputed master of masquerade, the reef fish that can make itself completely invisible on the sea floor, is the repulsive-looking scorpionfish (*Scorpaena*), a member of a dangerous tribe that includes the most venomous of all finned creatures, the stonefish. Lying in wait for prey, the stonefish looks exactly like a rock or a lump of algae-covered coral until it raises its 13 dorsal spines, each one packing enough venom to kill a fish—or a man unlucky enough to step on it.

Not all reef fish are venomous, although most are predators that feed in a highly organized chain. Their defensive faculties include camouflage and speed and also such special equipment as the tough forward dorsal fin of the triggerfish. The fish takes refuge in a reef recess, then locks the fin in place and wedges itself in so tightly that pursuing predators cannot dislodge it. With armorlike scales and tough, thick lips, the triggerfish feeds on sea urchins, adroitly avoiding the prickly defenses by tipping an urchin over on its back and attacking its soft underside. The deformed-looking anglerfish lures prey by extending a wand tipped with an inviting nodule of its own flesh. When a smaller fish strikes at the fleshy bait, the anglerfish, like a high-powered vacuum cleaner, sucks the victim into its mouth. If its prey should snatch off the bait, the anglerfish quickly grows another lure.

Such grotesque creatures as the stonefish and the anglerfish are contrasts in the brilliant kaleidoscope of the reef. Many of the reef dwellers are works of colorful abstract art: the graceful Moorish idols with white and black markings and lazily trailing elongated dorsal fins; the iridescent, fast-moving snappers; the hawkfish with a skin of scarlet plaid; the short-beaked parrotfish with a Joseph's coat of many colors, which feeds on the algae-covered limestone casing of the reef-building corals and converts it into fine-grained sand; the larger bumpfish, which also chews out great chunks of reef; the candy-striped squirrelfish; the sleekly gleaming, menacing-looking barracuda and the rainbow-hued wrasses.

Without its flamboyant troupe of fish, a coral reef would be merely a handsomely decorated stage. With them, it becomes an extravaganza.

Blue king angelfish

98

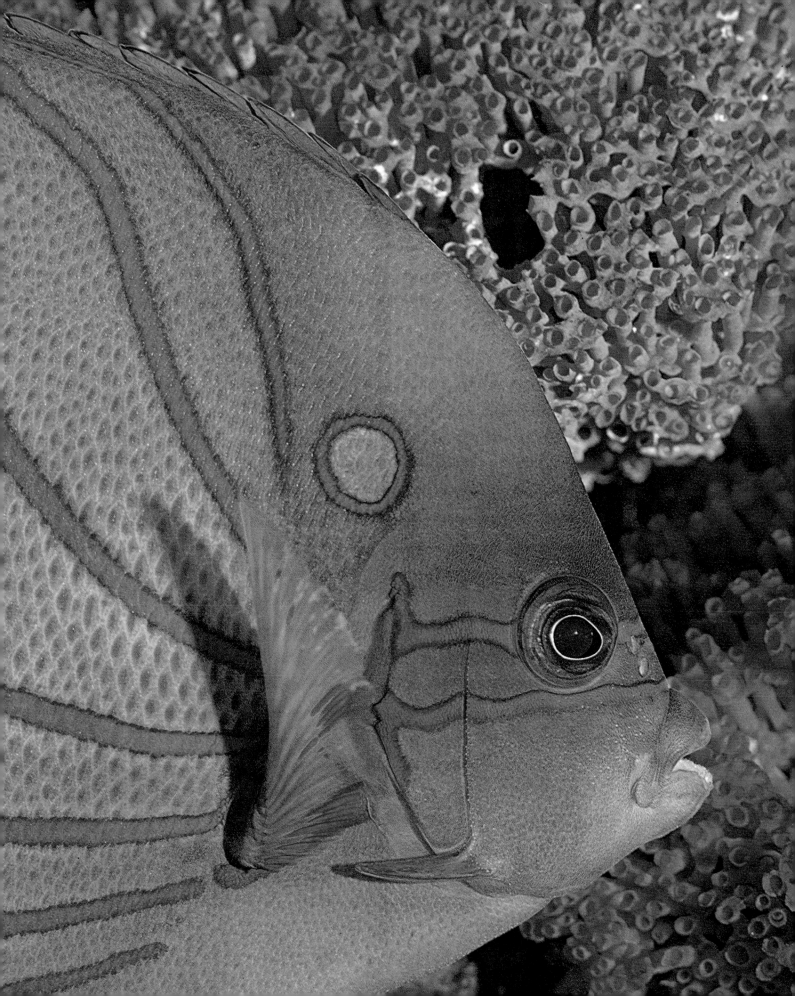

Band of Angels

The slender, coin-shaped fish of the family Chaetodontidae are among the most colorful reef dwellers. They are divided into two groups by the absence or presence of a spine on the lower rim of the cheekbone. Angelfish have such a spine—clearly visible in the picture of the queen angelfish above—but the appendage is lacking in butterflyfish (pages 104–105).

Most angelfish are shallow-water inhabitants that feed on small crustaceans, algae, worms and polyps. Identifying these fish by their color can be tricky, since the young of many species go through dramatic changes as they mature and may thus bear only a degree of resemblance to the adults. One such species is the French angelfish. By the time it reaches adulthood, the handsome youngster (opposite) will lose its yellow stripes and assume the more somber adult coloration: black scales edged with yellow. Similarly, the gray angelfish (left, center) once resembled the young French angelfish but now wears the lightly dappled scales of an adult.

Gray angelfish are found in West Indies waters and may grow up to one foot in length. Much smaller is the four-inch Potter's angelfish (left, bottom), a beautifully colored inhabitant of the Indo-Pacific oceans.

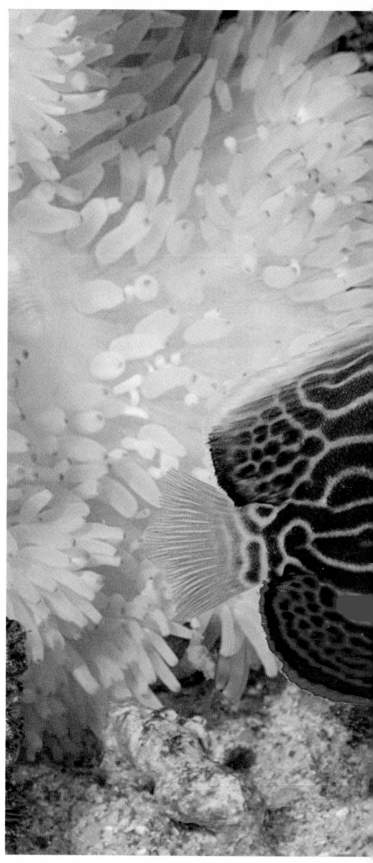

A young emperor angelfish waits tranquilly (right) as a cleaner shrimp curries its mouth for parasites. Within a period of weeks the emperor angel's juvenile coloration of deep blue with curving white stripes will gradually change into the adult pattern (above, top) of purple with contrasting longitudinal stripes of chrome yellow. Although they also have striped adult patterns, the Taiwan angelfish (above, center) and the regal angelfish (above, bottom) bear no resemblance to each other or to the emperor angel. All three live around the reefs of the Indo-Pacific oceans.

Deep-sea Butterflies

Close cousins of the angelfish, butterflyfish are the smaller members of the family Chaetodontidae, usually growing no longer than six to eight inches. Butterflyfish are very appropriately named. Not only do they exhibit color combinations and patterns as marvelous as those of their insect namesakes, they also have a comparable gift of extremely agile and graceful movement. Butterflyfish are expert swimmers, capable of darting about with ease through the labyrinthine maze of the coral reef. Their bodies, like those of angelfish, are as flat as pancakes, allowing them not only a high degree of maneuverability but also an effective means of camouflage. When seen from the front (as in the photograph of the copperband butterflyfish at left) these fish are reed-thin and blend in readily with algae and whiplike soft corals.

Lemon butterflyfish are one of the few species of butterflyfish that gather together to feed amiably in groups (opposite). Most, like the foureye butterflyfish (above), travel generally in pairs and establish a specific feeding territory, which they defend aggressively against intrusion by other butterflyfish—even those of the same species. Against predators, the foureye butterflyfish has evolved an effective passive defense; the second set of "eyes" near its tail often confuses an attacker long enough to allow the fish to get away.

Cattle of the Sea

Their habit of banding together in loosely knit herds as they graze over the hills and valleys of the reef in search of food has earned the radiantly colored parrotfish the name "cattle of the sea." The stoplight parrotfish (opposite) and the princess parrotfish (below) are herbivorous, like all of their kind, feeding on algae that grow on the coral. In order to get at their food, however, the fish must scrape the surface of the coral with their beaklike jaws and fused plates of teeth, which are excellent cutting and chiseling tools. Though they leave gashes in the coral surface, parrotfish return the scrapings, after they have digested them, to the coral environment in the form of sand.

Parrotfish, which are generally day feeders, usually rest at night. Some enclose themselves in a protective mucuslike wrapping (right); the process of fashioning their transparent sleeping bags takes some species about 30 minutes.

Defensive Weaponry

Every tropical sea on earth has its resident population of surgeonfish, peaceful, plant-eating creatures capable of color changes that vary their appearance according to their mood or the time of day.

Despite their unaggressive natures, however, surgeonfish are not to be treated lightly; when they are threatened or provoked, they can defend themselves handily with the scalpel-sharp spines they carry on either side of the base of their tails. In many species, such as the lollipop tang (below) and the Achilles and blue tangs (opposite), the spines are usually concealed in sheaths in the sides of the fish's body, which appear like miniature switchblades as the fish curves its body. Some species of surgeonfish have spines that are immovable and are always extended. The black sailfin's blade (opposite) is quite visible here but usually lies in a sheath. All these spines are extremely sharp and can inflict deep wounds in the sides of incautious fish and the hands of unwary fishermen.

Achilles tang

Sailfin tang·

Blue tang

Black sailfin tang

Yellow-eye tang

Groom Service

The wrasses are a large family of several hundred kinds of brightly colored fish, such as the red-tailed wrasse (below), that inhabit tropical reefs and temperate waters. They range in size from a pencil-thin, three-inch species to a five-foot-long giant weighing more than a hundred pounds. Most wrasses are identifiable by their well-developed front teeth that often protrude and which they sometimes use to slaughter invertebrates.

Many of the smaller wrasses belong to a group known as cleaner fish. Cleaners are usually found in one particular spot—near a patch of sand or a prominent rock—to which other, larger fish, such as groupers, snappers and par-rotfish, regularly come for the services the cleaners provide. These include removing parasites from a fish's scales and biting away dead tissue and bacteria from eyes, fins and gills. A Hawaiian cleaner wrasse is seen opposite grooming an Achilles tang. In return for its services the wrasse gets a good meal and, usually, immunity from the larger predators.

The cleaner fish seem to be highly valued by their clientele. Groups of fish often congregate around a particular cleaning station, waiting their turn. In general, cleaners are tireless workers. One was observed ministering to some 300 fish over a period of six hours.

Getting Along Swimmingly

Dorsal fins trailing like the lateen-rigged sails of Arabic dhows, a fleet of "Poor man's Moorish idols" investigates a reef (left) in the everlasting search for food. In their midst are several smaller lemon butterflyfish, inexplicably indifferent to the larger fish. Ichthyologists call the pictured gathering an aggregation, an assemblage of fish that travels in random groups for feeding, breeding or spawning.

Besides clustering in aggregations, fish swim either as solitary loners or in pairs or as members of schools or pods. Pods are dense masses of fish, swimming so closely together that their bodies touch. In schools, which may number a million or more members, the fish swim in the disciplined formation of naval convoys, lined up in precise ranks and separated by exact swimming distances, like the shimmering school of silversides, or hardy heads (overleaf). Some 4,000 species of fish swim in schools, or shoals, and the knack of schooling is instinctive: Young hatchlings begin to swim together when they are only a few days old, and the school becomes a distinct entity with no leaders and no individuals. When danger threatens, the entire school instantly wheels and changes course; the leading edge becomes a flank and a flank the leading edge. Besides offering the protection of numbers, schools make it much easier for fish to find mates and, often, food. How fish manage to school and what it is that keeps schools from turning into disorganized hordes are mysteries that are as deep as the sea itself.

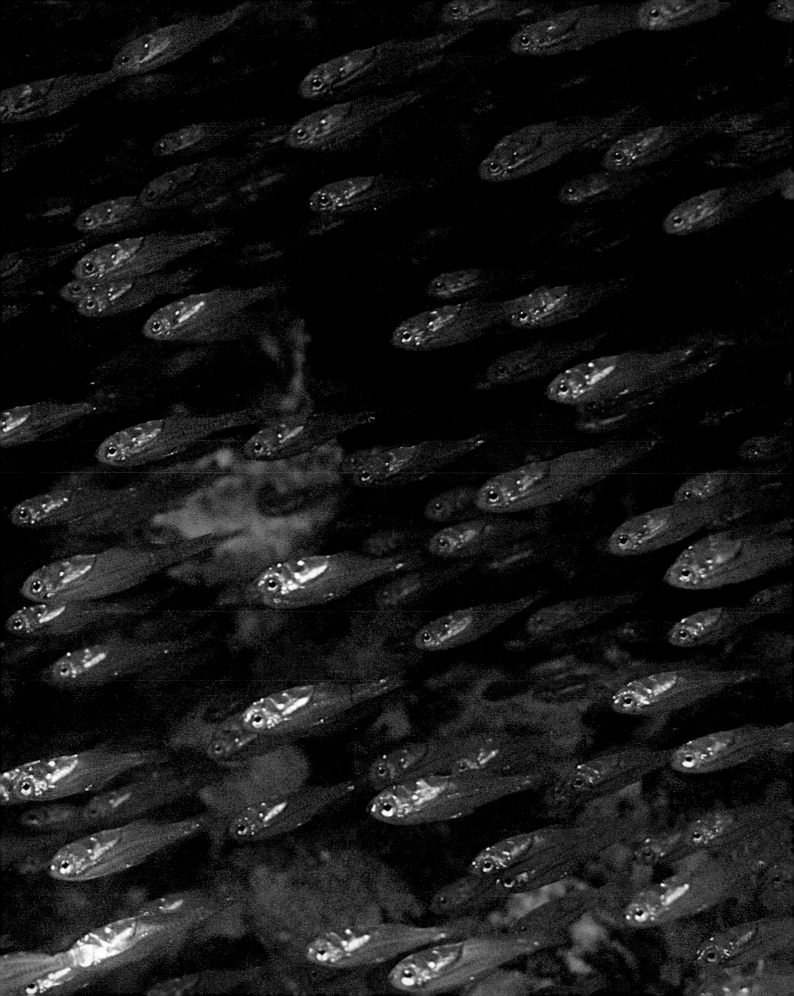

Hide and Seek

The sandy beds of the coral reef are the home of the yellowhead jawfish (above), the goby (left) and the garden eel (opposite). All three fish base their food-gathering activities in the safety of burrows, which they dig in the soft, gravelly surface. Garden eels and jawfish dig vertical burrows. The jawfish lines its shaft with bits of rock and coral for reinforcement; the eel secretes a slime from a gland in its tail that binds grains of sand together and provides a neat, unobstructed entry into its burrow. Both fish usually hover vertically above the bottom. The eels keep their tails tucked inside their holes, swaying to and fro as they feed on zooplankton from the water swirling around them. But at the first sign of danger they disappear, tail first, deep into their refuges.

Unlike the eels and jawfish, the goby shares its hole with a shrimp, seen tagging alongside the fish at left. The shrimp is nearly blind and maintains its constant contact with the goby by touch. While the shrimp is responsible for keeping the hole intact by constant shoveling and hauling, the goby is a seeing-eye guardian, positioning itself at the entrance to the burrow. When danger approaches the goby flees into the tunnel, alerting the shrimp, which follows right behind.

Safety Amid Death

In the crowded and often competitive world of the coral reef, numerous symbiotic relationships exist that mutually benefit two or more species living together. One of the most fascinating is the association between the strikingly marked anemonefish, pictured here, and the lethal sea anemones. The fish lay their eggs near the base of the sea anemones and rear their young among the swaying tentacles, straying from safety only to search for food.

Their host, the anemone, has fingerlike projections that are lined with stinging cells called nematocysts. These cells explode at the slightest touch, secreting a venom that immobilizes most small fish—except anemonefish. Several theories have been advanced to explain this immunity. The most widely accepted holds that anemonefish acquire a slimy substance from the anemone itself that makes it immune to the sting of the nematocysts. In return for their protection, the anemones receive morsels of food from the anemonefish, which may also serve as bait to lure other fish into the anemone's deadly arms.

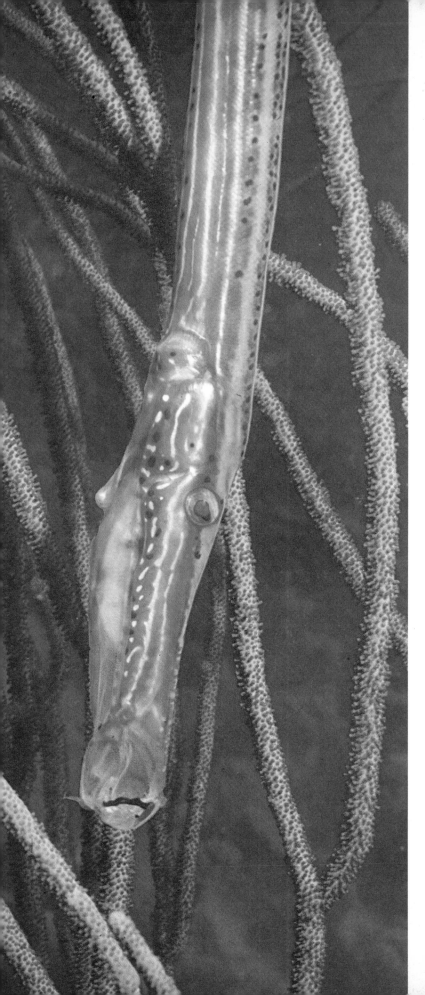

Evasive Inaction

Slow-swimming creatures like the trumpetfish pictured on this page, or sedentary, largely immobile ones like the scorpionfish opposite, have developed curious modes of camouflage that help them elude predators and surprise prey. Trumpetfish, like the *Aulostomus maculatus* at left, with their slender, elongated bodies and dappled coloring, often drift inconspicuously, head downward, among the boughs of soft coral. Some trumpetfish (below) frequent coral beds, where they blend well with the smoldering pink corals. Trumpetfish are also adept at sidling up to a parrotfish or grouper and swimming alongside under the protection of the larger fish. When the pair nears one of the crustaceans, worms or smaller fish eaten by trumpetfish —but avoided by their swimming companions—the trumpetfish suddenly swims away. With a swift intake of water through its long, flexible snout, it literally inhales its prey. Trumpetfish share this feeding method with pipefish and seahorses, all members of the order of tube-mouthed fish.

The scorpionfish (opposite) is almost invisible as it lies half buried in the sand, waiting for its prey to happen by. The swimmer who steps on one not only punctures his foot on its spines but forces toxin from the spines into his foot—an agonizing though rarely fatal experience.

Delivery Boys

The two creatures pictured on these pages are males, and they are "pregnant." They are members of the bizarre-looking order of tube-mouthed fish, some of which carry role reversal of the sexes to an extreme. Though the order is named for horselike snouts that the fish utilize with pinpoint accuracy to suck in food, their reproductive behavior is even more remarkable. The female's function is limited to depositing her eggs in the male's kangaroolike pouch, seen clearly in the bulging paunch of the giant seahorse below and on the gondola-shaped underbelly of the pipefish at right. The male fertilizes the eggs as they enter the pouch and incubates them for eight to 10 days before giving live birth. The pipefish bears his young with little difficulty, but those who have observed the contortions of the male seahorse as the tiny (no bigger than five eighths of an inch) babies emerge speculate that he may actually undergo labor pains.

Three seahorses anchor themselves against underwater currents by hooking onto coral with their prehensile tails. Some two dozen seahorse species inhabit the world's oceans, the adults ranging in size from one and a half to eight inches. For motive power, seahorses are equipped with a small dorsal fin midway down their backs, a tiny flaplike pectoral fin on either side behind the head and a bit of fin tissue beneath the abdominal bulge. But even though the fins may flutter rapidly, seahorses are extremely slow swimmers, requiring up to five minutes to scull a distance of three feet.

125

Credits

Cover—J. Burton, Bruce Coleman, Inc. 1—Dr. Richard H. Chesher, Photo Researchers, Inc. 5—Z. Leszczynski, Animals Animals. 6–7—J. Dominis, Time Inc. 9—H. Genthe, Sea Library. 12—C. Ray, P.R., Inc. 14–15—G. Cahan, P. R., Inc. 16–17—J. Dominis, Time Inc. 19—Wolfgang Bayer. 20—George Silk. 21 (top)—R.R. Abrams, B.C., Inc.; (bottom)—C. Newbert, B.C., Inc. 22—C. Nicklin, Woodfin Camp. 22–23—S. Keiser, Sea Library. 24, 25,—C. Roessler, Sea Library. 32 (left)—M.T. O'Keefe, B.C., Inc.; (top, right)—C. Newbert, B.C., Inc.; (bottom, right)—Dr. R.H. Chesher, P.R., Inc. 33—Dr. R.H. Chesher, P.R., Inc. 34–35—D. Reed, Sea Library. 36–37—C. Roessler, Sea Library. 38–39—J. Jones, P.R., Inc. 39—C. Newbert, B.C., Inc. 40—J. Boland, Sea Library. 41, 43—Z. Leszczynski, Animals Animals. 44—C. Roessler, Sea Library. 45 (top)—C. Newbert, B.C.; Inc., (bottom)—N. Sefton, P.R., Inc. 46 (top)—C. Nicklin, Woodfin Camp; (bottom)—C. Newbert, B.C., Inc. 47, 49—Z. Leszczynski, Animals Animals. 50—C. Newbert, B.C., Inc. 51—Dr. R.H. Chesher, P.R., Inc. 52 (top)—C. Newbert, B.C., Inc.; (bottom)—J. Van der Walt, Sea Library. 53—Z. Leszczynski, Animals Animals. 55—J. Dominis, Time Inc. 56—W. Curtsinger, P.R., Inc. 58—Z. Leszczynski, Animals Animals. 58–59—Dr. R.H. Chesher, P.R., Inc. 60—J. Boland, Sea Library. 61–65—Z. Leszczynski, Animals Animals. 66–67—K. Lucas, P.R., Inc. 67—Dr. R.H. Chesher, P.R., Inc. 70 (top)—Dr. R.H. Chesher, P.R., Inc.; (bottom)—R. Evans, Sea Library. 71—C. Newbert, B.C., Inc. 72—Z. Leszczynski, Animals Animals. 73, 75—C. Roessler, Sea Library. 76—Dr. R.H. Chesher, P.R., Inc. 77—J. Jones, P.R., Inc. 80 (top)—N. Sefton, P.R., Inc., P. Capen, Sea Library. 81—J. Boland, Sea Library. 82 (top)—C. Roessler, Sea Library; (bottom)—C. Roessler, Animals Animals. 83—C. Roessler, Animals Animals. 85—R. Chesher, P.R., Inc. 86—J. Burton, B.C., Inc. 87—J. Carmichael, B.C., Inc. 88—W.H. Amos, B.C., Inc. 89—R.N. Mariscal, B.C., Inc. 90–91—C. Roessler, Sea Library. 92 (left)—J. Carmichael, B.C., Inc.; (right)—Ron & Valerie Taylor, B.C., Inc. 93 (top)— J. Burton, B.C., Inc.; (center)—D. Reed, Sea Library; (bottom)—A. Power, P.R., Inc. 94—C. Roessler, Sea Library. 95—Z. Leszczynski, Animals Animals. 96 (top, left)—C. Newbert, B.C., Inc.; (middle, left)—W. Harvey, P.R., Inc.; (bottom, left)—W.M. Stephen B.C., Inc. 96 (right)—Z. Leszczynski, Animals Animals. 97 (top)—C. Roessler, Sea Library; (bottom)—P. Faulkes, Sea Library. 99—T. McHugh for Steinhart Aquarium, P.R., Inc. 100 (top)—C. Roessler, Sea Library; (center)—R. Kinne, P.R., Inc.; (bottom)—Z. Leszczynski, Animals Animals. 101—C. Roessler, Sea Library. 102 (top)—C. Roessler, Sea Library; (center and bottom)—Z. Leszczynski, Animals Animals. 102–103—Z. Leszczynski, Animals Animals. 104 (left)—J. Burton, B.C., Inc.; (right)—N. Sefton, P.R., Inc. 105—E. Robinson, Sea Library. 106—Dr. R.H. Chesher, P.R., Inc. 107 (top)—W.A. Starck, Sea Library; (bottom)—C. Roessler, Sea Library. 108–111—Z. Leszczynski, Animals Animals. 112–113—C. Roessler, Sea Library. 114–115—V. Taylor, B.C., Inc. 116 (top)—S. Bisserot, B.C., Inc.; (bottom)—R. Chesher, P.R., Inc. 117—A. Power, B.C., Inc. 118—Z. Leszczynski, Animals Animals. 119 (top)—R. Mariscal, B.C., Inc.; (bottom)—C. Roessler, Sea Library. 120 (left)—R. Chesher, P.R., Inc.; (right)—C. Roessler, Sea Library. 121—Wolfgang Bayer. 122—Jen & Des Bartlett, B.C., Inc. 122–123—Jen & Des Bartlett, B.C. Inc. 124–125—Oxford Scientific Films, B.C., Inc.

Photographs on endpapers are used courtesy of Time-Life Picture Agency and Russ Kinne and Stephen Dalton of Photo Researchers, Inc. and Nina Leen.

Film sequence on page 11 is from "Hunters in the Reef", a program in the Time-Life Television series *Wild, Wild World of Animals*. MAP on page 10 is by Francis and Shaw, Inc. ILLUSTRATIONS on pages 27–31 by John Groth; the illustration on page 69 by André Durenceau; the illustration on page 79 is by Dr. Fritz Riedl.

Bibliography

NOTE: Asterisk at the left means that a paperback volume is also available.

*Arnold, Augusta Foote, *The Sea at Ebb Tide*. Dover Publications, 1968.

Barnett, Lincoln, "The Coral Reef." *Life*, February 8, 1954, pp. 74–94.

Buchsbaum, Ralph, and Milne, Lorus J., *The Lower Animals*. Doubleday, 1962.

Campbell, Andrew C., *The Coral Seas*. Putnam, 1976.

*Carson, Rachel, *The Edge of the Sea*. Houghton, Mifflin, 1955.

Chesher, Richard H., "Hidden Animals of the Sea." *Oceans*, August 1969, pp. 53–59.

*Clarke, Arthur C., *The Treasure of the Great Reef*. Harper & Row, 1964.

Cousteau, Jacques-Yves and Diole, Philippe, *Life and Death in a Coral Sea*. Doubleday, 1971.

Cromie, William J., *The Living World of the Sea*. Prentice-Hall, 1966.

Darwin, Charles, *The Structure and Distribution of Coral Reefs*. University of California Press, 1962.

Dozier, Thomas, *Dangerous Sea Creatures*. Time-Life Films, 1976.

Engel, Leonard, *The Sea*. Time-Life Books, 1972.

Grzimek, Bernhard, *Grzimek's Animal Life Encyclopedia*, Vols. 1, 3, 4, 5. Van Nostrand Reinhold, 1968, 1973.

Hedgepath, J.W., ed., *Treatise on Marine Ecology and Paleontology*, Vol. 1. Waverly Press, 1957.

Hentig, Roland von, *The Coral World*. BBC, 1973.

Herald, Earl S., *Living Fishes of the World*. Doubleday, 1971.

McGregor, Craig, *The Great Barrier Reef*. Time-Life International, 1973.

National Audubon Society, *Life on a Coral Reef*. Doubleday, 1969.

Randall, John E., *Caribbean Reef Fishes*. T.F.H. Publications, 1968.

*Ricciuti, Edward R., *Killers of the Sea*. Walker, 1973.

Sale, Peter F., "Reef Fish Lottery." *Natural History*, February, 1976, pp. 61–65.

Silverberg, Robert, *The World of Coral*. Duell, Sloan and Pearce, 1965.

Sisson, Robert F., "Life Cycle of a Coral." *National Geographic*, June, 1973, pp. 780–793.

Smith, F.G., *Atlantic Reef Corals*. University of Miami Press, 1971.

Stoddart, D.R., "Variations on a Coral Theme." *Geographic Magazine*, June, 1971, pp. 610–615.

Yonge, C.M., *A Year on the Great Barrier Reef*. Putnam, 1930.

Zann, Leon P., "Symbionts of Sea Fans and Sea Whips." *Oceans*, No. 1, 1977, pp. 10–15.

Zeiller, Warren, *Tropical Marine Invertebrates of Southern Florida and the Bahama Islands*. John Wiley, 1974.

Index

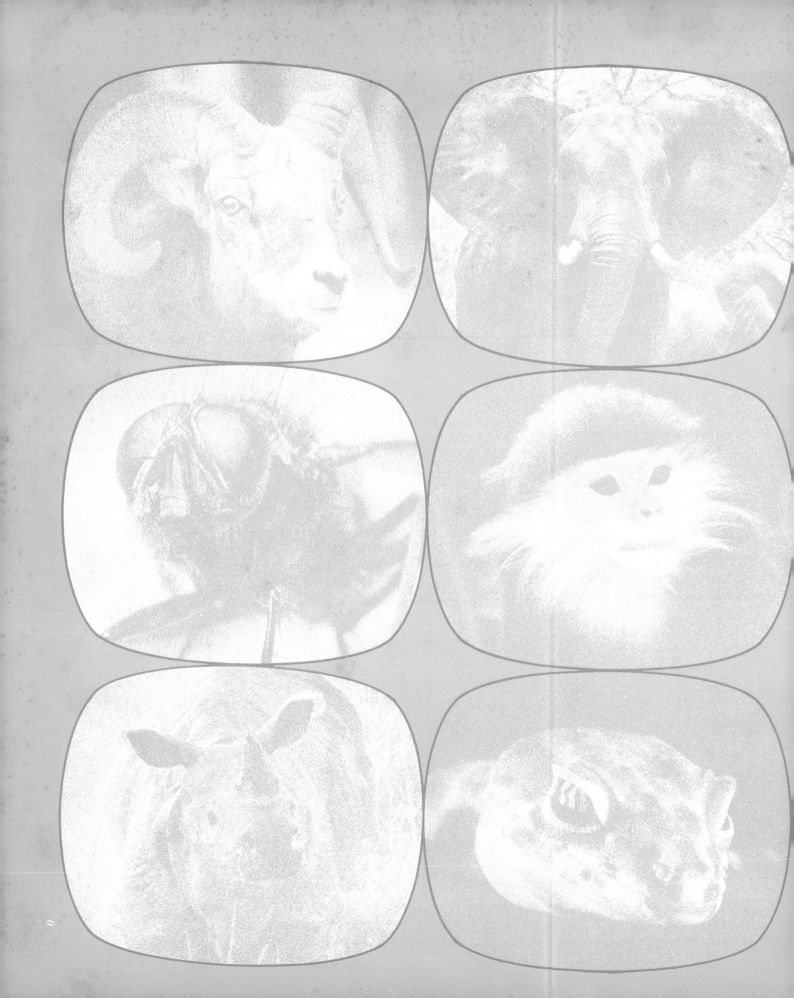